— Land of — Strangers

—Ash Amin—

polity

First published in 2012 by Polity Press

Polity Press
65 Bridge Street
Cambridge CB2 1UR, UK

Polity Press
350 Main Street
Malden, MA 02148, USA

ISBN-13: 978-0-7456-5217-7
ISBN-13: 978-0-7456-5218-4(pb)

A catalogue record for this book is available from the British Library.

Typeset in 11 on 13 pt Sabon
by Toppan Best-set Premedia Limited
Printed and bound in Great Britain by MPG Books Group Limited

The publisher has used its best endeavours to ensure that the URLs for external websites referred to in this book are correct and active at the time of going to press. However, the publisher has no responsibility for the websites and can make no guarantee that a site will remain live or that the content is or will remain appropriate.

Every effort has been made to trace all copyright holders, but if any have been inadvertently overlooked the publisher will be pleased to include any necessary credits in any subsequent reprint or edition.

For further information on Polity, visit our website: www.politybooks.com

Contents

Acknowledgements

Many people have influenced the thinking in this book, but some in particular I wish to thank for their ideas and generosity: Louise Amoore, Ben Anderson, Laura Balbo, Les Back, Madeleine Bunting, Michel Callon, Iain Chambers, Patrick Cohendet, Steve Graham, Gernot Grabher, Colin McFarlane, Eduardo Mendieta, Greg Noble, Adi Ophir, Edgar Pieterse, Kapil Raj, Arun Saldanha, Saskia Sassen, AbdouMaliq Simone, Susan Smith, David Stark, Pep Subirós, and Amanda Wise. I am also grateful to Bhikhu Parekh, Richard Sennett and Nigel Thrift for finding the time to read the book. My special thanks to Nigel for years of friendship and wise counsel. My doctoral students, Jonathan Darling, Michele Lancione, Dan Swanton and Helen Wilson, have been a source of inspiration and help. They have kept me thinking. I also thank Joanne Roberts (and *Research Policy*) for allowing me to draw on our joint work for chapter 2, the editors of *Theory, Culture and Society* for permission to reprint chapter 4, and of *City* for extracts from two of my articles published in 2007 and 2008 to enable me to write chapter 3. At Polity, John Thompson and Jennifer Jahn have been characteristically graceful, while the quality of comment from the two anonymous readers who were sent the first draft prompted me to rewrite well over half the original typescript. The book started its life at Durham University, gathered pace during a glorious fellowship in 2011 at the Swedish Collegium of Advanced Study (SCAS) in Uppsala, and drew to completion at Cambridge University. My thanks to colleagues at the formidable Department of Geography at Durham and at the Institute of Advanced Study that I had the privilege to lead until August 2011, to Bjorn Wittrock and Barbro Klein at SCAS who created the opening for this book to come to realization, and to Sue Owens and other wonderful new colleagues for welcoming me warmly to the Department of Geography at Cambridge. This book is for an idea – that the stranger is neither friend nor foe, but constitutive. It is also for my family – Lynne, Usha, Sam and Isla. I dedicate it to Josep Ramoneda for the courage he showed in engaging with the stranger. He paid the price for it.

Introduction

Modern Western societies have become thoroughly hybrid in every sense. With their heterogeneous populations and cultures, they exist as gatherings of strangers – home grown and migrant. Yet the grip of the imaginary that each society exists as a homeland with its own people, known and loyal to itself (and distinct from strangers from another land) remains vice-like. But could it be that if cosmopolitan societies hold together, they do so around plural publics and as the result of active work by collective institutions, integrating technologies, and constructed narratives and feelings of togetherness, rather than around givens of historic community?

Indeed, modern Western societies consist of so many spatial provenances, from the local and national to the virtual, postcolonial and transnational, that there can be no certainty of the whereabouts of the givens of historic community, which still remains widely understood as a territorially defined entity. In turn, if the locations of community (and its outside) spill over beyond its traditional containers, so too does the constituency of social being. Modern humans are more than flesh, feeling and consciousness, formed as social animals and civic subjects by a myriad of other material inputs, from technological objects to transplants and prosthetics. The habit of seeing humans as divorced from nature and technology continues to persist, allowing easy distinctions to be made between some subjects as pure and others a impure, some as citizens and others as strangers.

This book focuses on what goes on in the gap – in the West between – the narratives or practices of societal singularity and those of pluralism, affecting the chances of those labelled as strangers or minorities. My argument is that the fate of the stranger lies in the play between hybrid and singular performances and projections of the social. I do not see this necessarily as the conflict between everyday life, understood as the sphere of freedom and opportunity, and the machinery of societal governance, understood as the sphere of restraint and discipline. Each sphere consists of both kinds of social practice, for example, in the sphere of everyday life the persistence of legacies of racial judgement that return some strangers as outsiders and threats, or in the sphere of representation and rule descriptions of the stranger as co-habitant and potential citizen.

It is the gap itself between singularity and plurality that interests me, as the space in which some humans become labelled as insiders or outsiders, publics and nations define themselves as hybrid or otherwise, and the stranger is or is not afforded air to breathe. My interest in this space stems from a desire to widen contemporary discussion on the fate of the stranger in Western societies, in two senses especially. First, with its focus on the racialized Other, the book examines the multiple ways in which the stranger is construed as an outsider: the object of ejection, domestication or tolerance. It uncovers an intricate and often interwoven set of biopolitical, behavioural and affective forces that are simultaneously ingrained and unstable. Accordingly, second, the book expands the case for the society of strangers, looking for openings in the overlay between everyday hybridity and hegemonic disjuncture, gathered into an explicit politics of multiplicity and common cause to justify the diverse society.

A prime reason for the desire to expand debate on the society of strangers is to push back at an increasingly narrow scholarly and policy framing of the challenges of social integration and cohesion under conditions of hyper-diversity. My argument is that, in seeing too much of the human in the social and in expecting too much from the inter-human in resolving social difference and antagonism, a narrow framing misrecognizes the society of strangers compositionally and in terms of its normative potential. If, in the latter half of the twentieth century, socialist, feminist, queer and postcolonial thought pressed for, and succeeded in legitimating, a vision of the diverse and open society as a community of equals allowed to express and exercise their difference but united in common cause, the twenty-first century has begun with narratives of common life based on reduced or reconciled differences and strengthened social and community ties.

A logic of the communal as the field of interpersonal and intercultural ties, underwritten by shared historic values, has come to the fore (Vertovec and Wessendorf, 2010), spurred by negative commentary on multiculturalism in the wake of 9/11, including accusations that strangers and minorities expect too much and give back too little, make majorities feel like strangers in their own land, and weaken social cohesion by undermining national heritage and tradition. Envisaging the good society as the society of responsible citizens and collaborating communities, this logic recommends the exclusion or domestication of the stranger, the revival of core national values, and the strengthening of ties among and between communities. This book judges such a turn to be regressive and unrealistic: regressive for its veiled xenophobia and exclusionary nostalgia, and unrealistic for its denial of the plural constituency of modern being and belonging.

This turn is judged to be no casual invention, but one drawing on a long line of sociological inquiry interested in the nature and role of social ties in the modern society. For at least a century, the social sciences have judged modernity by its impact on social and community ties, generally understood to have been weakened by the proliferation of many material, technological and institutional intermediaries. While some observers have found in this displacement an opportunity for society to look beyond the limitations of tradition and bounded community, others have judged it to suppress collective progress and social cohesion. The balance of opinion has varied with circumstance and context, and our times, viewed as a time of extreme societal fluidity in an insecure and unstable world, seem to be favouring once again a yearning for the society of mutual obligations and strong social ties.

The virtues of community are being rediscovered in diverse fields of social organization. For example, work on the economy, backed by policy work on social capital and on communities of practice, increasingly argues that factors such as trust, loyalty and mutuality are important lubricants of market transactions and vital sources of learning, creativity and innovation. Similarly, work on cohesion in a fast-moving and cosmopolitan world has turned to the steadying hand of interpersonal and communal ties in dealing with the challenges of anomie, indifference and aversion. So too with discussion of citizenship in the open and mixed society, which is increasingly framed as a requirement of duty and conformity (especially from strangers and minorities), rather than as a right or entitlement. In the same way, in cultural studies, the public sphere is being redefined as the space of encounter and reconciliation, instead of being seen as a field shaped by the interaction between diverse publics and counter-publics. Across these strands, we see the social reduced to the communal, and potentiality to the powers of association and collective identification.

This book seeks to both extend and supersede such a resurgent sociology of ties. Echoing the latter's focus on the relational and co-constituted nature of social life, the book turns to the phenomenology of everyday experience, including the nature of social interaction, to explain cultural habits and norms, instead of presuming them to be already given to particular bodily forms, individual and collective. Here, the entanglements of situated practice are taken seriously by interrogating the multiple provenances of judgement that envelope the event – mediated and direct, immediate and remote, purposeful and unintentional, cognitive and non-cognitive, archived and actual. The meeting of strangers is considered to involve much more than the bodily moment, or, for that matter, the phenomenology of social connectivity.

Interpreting the encounter, and more generally habits of living among others, as the space in which the pre-formed, performed and imagined intersect to mould social dispositions and feelings (Vertovec, 2011), some of the sites of celebratory writing on social ties are revisited. With its expanded reading of situated practice, this study explains trust in the workplace – and related outcomes such as learning and creativity – as an always fragile and cultivated art born out of joint work, shared goals and standards, craft practices, and technological alignment, rather than as the gift of particular forms of social disposition. If strangers become collaborators and co-creators it is through particular forms of labour that generate trust, and not the reverse. Similarly, the book argues that public feelings of empathy or aversion towards the stranger are not reducible to the intensities of social interaction or the qualities of collective culture. Instead, they are shown to be instantiations of a slew of personal and collective labelling conventions – inherited, learnt, absorbed and practised – that flow into the moment of encounter, but that are regulated by cognitive and sensory judgements stimulated by the specifics of the occasion.

Here, the practices of situated judgement are interpreted as temporally freighted, multispatial, and materially formed: the realization of many provinces of cultural formation. Accordingly, a central claim, following Latour's

(2005) interpretation of the social as the field of human and non-human association, is that the turn towards the interpersonal as the measure of community offers an overly restrictive account. In contrast, effort is made to recognize the bodies, objects, technologies, legacies, ideas and imaginaries – tensely held together in relational space – that shape the affective proximities of humans to their worlds and with each other. Human being and belonging are shown to be intensely mediated and hybrid, even when seemingly singular and unambiguous. Convinced that 'foregrounding material factors and reconfiguring our very understanding of matter are prerequisites for any plausible account of coexistence and its conditions in the twenty-first century' (Coole and Frost, 2010: 2), the book brings into play bodily affects, inscribed legacies, biopolitical regimes and classificatory conventions to explain dispositions towards, and among, strangers. It introduces urban technologies, infrastructures and aesthetics to explain negotiations of difference in public space, ornaments, prosthetics and intimate publics to explain pathologies of care, projects, protocols and technologies of assembly to explain workplace intimacies, and models and projections of the future to explain the fervours of community.

The purpose of this reconsideration of the phenomenology of the encounter is to dislodge the politics of belonging from its current mooring in a discourse of strong social ties. A first aim is to recognize cares and responsibilities formed in material, technological, symbolic and imagined space (and with nature and animals, although this dimension is not covered in the book – see Mendieta, 2011, on how a genuine politics of co-habitation requires empathy with vulnerable co-species). Such intimacies are considered as allies rather than obstacles in a politics of human intimacy, depending on whether crafts and cares cultivated in singular space (often antipathetic to strangers) can be extended as a form of interest in the commons, including the claims upon it of the stranger. It is proposed that the cultivation of labour, learning and living is a craft that requires continual attentiveness and care, such that empathy – for objects, projects, nature, the commons – can spread as a public sentiment that also serves to regulate feelings among strangers.

While the book finds no quarrel with a politics of care able to push back at the pathology of self that has become so prevalent in the contemporary West, it remains disturbed by the prospect that a politics of respectful distance, principled disagreement and common life becomes discarded as a way of negotiating the society of strangers. A second aim, therefore, is to defend a politics of difference formed around the impersonal, the openly disputed and the public. Two guiding principles are introduced to make such a politics inclusive. One is the principle of multiplicity, allowing all claims – settled and new, mainstream and alternative – to be rendered small, provisional and equivalent, pressed to make their case, accept the legitimacy of other claims, and build coalitions and synergies (Connolly, 2005). Public acceptance of this principle will help to render the strange familiar and the familiar strange, and collective life a constant negotiation of difference.

But such a public arena needs to be capable of harnessing collective commitments to ensure that pluralism does not degenerate into a free struggle that works in favour of the fittest. For this reason, the principle of the commons is recovered as a second staple of the society of strangers, intended as both an enabling public sphere and a provisioning collective resource. A case is made for a flourishing and dissenting public sphere, not only so that many publics can form and learn to accept the settlements of open play, but also so that shared affinities and interests can arise out of participation and engagement. A case is also made for returning to the social state – its public spaces, collective infrastructures, welfare protections, and social democratic traditions. However, no unqualified return is proposed. Recognizing the multiplicities of the open and negotiated society, the book accepts that the social state can fix only

so much through its tangible provisions and cultural persuasions, but it also maintains that without it there can be
no fair deal for the vulnerable and disadvantaged, including the stranger.

The openings and closures for the stranger in the gap
between singularity and pluralism are examined themati-
cally through six chapters. The first chapter summarizes
the contemporary turn towards community cohesion
through social ties, and goes on to explore the implications
of attachment formed with, and around, objects, technologies and common spaces such as friendship groups and
intimate publics formed around genre films or fiction.
Taking such attachments seriously, the chapter proposes
that a politics of care, aware of the limitations of interpersonal proximities, might usefully turn to strategies to rein-
force social interest in the shared material, virtual and
affective commons. It considers curatorial attention of the
zones of engagement with other humans and non-humans
to hold more promise for a politics of bridging difference
than is an ethic of care for the stranger or for a particular
notion of community.

Such curatorship is also proposed as the staple of economic innovation, the means by which strangers learn to
become creative collaborators in the workplace. The
second chapter examines the social dynamic of knowledge
generation in different situations of collaborative work
(e.g., craft workshops, scientific projects, virtual communities). It claims that learning and innovation, along with the
integration of peripheral participants into a creative community of practice, is the result of purposeful attention to
shared problems, sustained by expertise honed in application, alignment of diverse and distributed knowledge
inputs, and maintenance of an architecture and ethos of
joint effort. Trust, mutuality and obligation, claimed as the
sources of creativity (and cohesion) in work on social ties,
are explained as the product and not the cause of collaborative engagement. The chapter returns labour, joint work

and craft culture as key to social integration and economic creativity in the society of strangers.

The third chapter turns to everyday mingling in urban public space, to reappraise how co-presence shapes human dispositions and feelings. The history of sociology is peppered with claims about the decisive cultural and political significance of social interaction in urban public space. The negotiation of space shared with other strangers has been considered to have civilizing, imitative or alienating effects, depending on the sentiments aroused, ranging from enmity and indifference to guile and empathy. Such symptomatic readings have shaped many an urban intervention to alter the pattern of human contact in public space in order to change habits of living with difference. While reaffirming the proposition that in modernity human being and the negotiation of urban space are inextricably intertwined, the chapter turns to the urban habitat itself – the assembly of technologies, built forms, infrastructures, services, rules of order and symbolic landscapes that urban dwellers unthinkingly negotiate – to explain collective culture and social dispositions. Stranger relations are proposed to filter through this 'urban unconscious', rather than through habits of interpersonal contact in public space. Accordingly, the chapter outlines a politics of the stranger formed through the urban commons.

This is not to underestimate the freight of the bodily encounter, where the play of open interaction between strangers intersects with the performance of honed scripts of bodily classification. This theme is taken up in the fourth chapter through a discussion of the phenomenology of race; a choice influenced by the sharp escalation of racial labelling and consequent condemnation of the stranger since 9/11. It is argued that a complex machinery of inherited and instituted classificatory practices, symbolic persuasions, and social behaviours regulates the encounter, generally ensuring the continuity of familiar racial hierarchies despite the open hermeneutics of the situated encounter. But the chapter also acknowledges that the intensity of aversion or recognition varies temporally and spatially, closely regulated by biopolitical mobilizations of race in a given situation (shaped, for example, by state rules on migration and assimilation to media and political languages of community and its outsiders). Accordingly, the chapter leans towards an anti-racism focusing on the biopolitical environment, such that the harms of thought-free bodily judgements that invade the encounter can remain contained.

In an always difficult habitat of survival for the marked stranger, collective understanding of imagined community is of critical importance for the power it possesses to define who belongs and the terms of togetherness. This is the theme of the last two chapters. The fifth chapter dwells on the post-national, more precisely, the idea of Europe as a symbol of unity; a symbol freighted by a history of imperial hauteur but also universalist and progressive ambitions and today captured by resurgent nationalist sentiment against the unassimilated stranger. The chapter chooses to address the question of imagined community by focusing on the making of the European public sphere, a simultaneously weak and strong communicative and affective space. It reveals how circulating keywords and prevalent sentiments are spreading a noxious contagion of aversion towards the stranger, but it also argues that as an incomplete and ill-formed space, the European public sphere has the potential of sustaining a counter-narrative of engagement with the stranger. The chapter summarizes the contemporary uses of xenophobia in Europe before outlining its case – and requirements – for a public sentiment of unity that values openness and curiosity in facing an uncertain and turbulent future.

The power of contemporary projections of an uncertain future darkened by the strange and unknown, however, is not taken lightly. The last chapter examines the implications of a resurgent narrative in the West of the future as apocalyptic – out of control and heading towards catastrophe – and in need of warlike preparations, including the suspension of democracy and the elimination of the strange and impure. It is argued that a hitherto prevalent risk culture, banking on comprehensive insurance against the vicissitudes of a knowable future, is giving way to an understanding of the future as illegible, unstable and dangerous, and, for this, in need of constant vigilance and aggressive intervention. If the first culture offered qualified support to the stranger onshore, the second one is less accommodating in its selection of the subjects that count, indeed aggressive in its interventions to excise the destabilizing outside and the stranger who calls. Judging these developments as highly inflammatory, the book closes with a formulation of preparedness, open to all available resources and experiments of engagement at home and abroad, in order to anticipate the uncertain and turbulent future.

Like its reading of the social world, the style of the book is hybrid, combining multidisciplinary analysis with polemical and normative intent. The style may not please the reader looking for sustained disciplinary scholarship or a unitary theory of the subject. The choice, however, is guided by the urgency of the political moment. Frustrated with the current turn towards a politics of interpersonal and communitarian ties, and disappointed by the absence of a credible alternative that is bold about the virtues of the society of strangers, the approach adopted is to scan the landscape for evidence and proposals for new ways of gathering diversity into a functioning commons. The times press for a collage of ideas, illustrations and methods that show that multiplicity, solidarity and common provision remain valid principles to address a future that can only become more hybridized. To yearn for purity is to close off possibility.

− 1 −

The Freight of Social Ties

The face is the only location of community, the only possible city.

Agamben, 2000: 91[1]

Introduction

This chapter looks at the politics of community, more specifically, the widely held assumption today that the strength of interpersonal ties in a society has a direct bearing on its cohesiveness and the civic interest of its citizens. Those who hold this view interpret the continuing displacement of ties based on social familiarity, trust and local community by ties that are more self-serving, impersonal, dispersed and deferred (e.g., to states and markets) as problematic. Its dissenters argue, instead, that the sites and motivations of citizenship have simply changed, that the rise of impersonal and mediated networks of affiliation demand a different kind of politics of community. For them, the problem is one of optic, stemming from an overly humanist framing of contemporary social ties.

[1]From Giorgio Agamben, *Means without End: Notes on Politics,* trans. by Vincenzo Binetti and Cesare Casarino (University of Minnesota Press, 2000). Copyright 2000 by the Regents of the Unversity of Minnesota.

This chapter joins the dissenters, with a view to proposing a politics of social integration and cohesion truer to the material of contemporary social affiliation. It argues against an anthropomorphic interpretation of social connectivity, which yields inflated and unrealistic political expectations from societies characterized by multiple subjectivities and loyalties. Such interpretation, in posing local community and face-to-face communication as the antithesis of cosmopolitanism and virtual affiliation, is held to occlude other and hybrid geographies of attachment that lend themselves to a different kind of collective normative. Examining affinities formed in virtual space, through material objects, in intimate publics, and through friendship networks, the chapter proposes a scheme of social belonging and civic interest freed from the obligation of recognition among strangers.

Dualist Oppositions

Zygmunt Bauman (2000) has described ours as the age of liquid modernity, one characterized by a number of unsettlements. The first is the continual uprooting and displacement of peoples. A second is the slow creep of fear, anxiety and watchfulness into even the most intimate spaces as a sense of the world and home at risk takes root. A third is the displacement of collective cultures of identification by theologies of the self and specialist affiliation. A fourth is the weakening of traditional ties of homeland community, as individuals become members of multiple and technologically mediated networks of affiliation. For Bauman, a new world of fragile, ephemeral and dispersed affiliations is arising to replace traditional community ties, a prognosis endorsed by many similar accounts of human displacement linked to globalization, rising inequality, and risk and uncertainty.

Such thinking acknowledges that the impact of liquid modernity (or however else we may describe our times) on different social actors is variegated, shaped by social circumstances, location and individual capability. It accepts the differences in affiliation behaviour between the jetsetting professional loyal to no country, the migrant developing new connections and sustaining distant ties, the hapless indigene sheltering in tradition and heritage to cope with rising immigration, the believer taking comfort in religious community and dismayed by hyper-modernity and secularism, or the poor person left with only the immediacy of family and local ties.

Normative judgement on the world on the move, however, seems less encumbered by such nuance. Typically, as Tim Cresswell (2006) observes, reaction has been either 'sedentarist', yearning for the security of strong ties forged in defined communities and wary of a future without such affiliations, or 'nomadic', valuing mobility, exteriority and multiple ties, and elective affinities in the negotiation of difference. While the one looks back to territorial and interpersonal bonds, the other finds cause in cosmopolitan connections and other kinds of border crossing (Sennett, 2008a).

'Community' has returned as a keyword in sedentarist thinking, as the antidote for the failings of liquid modernity, reviving once again yearning for social unity based on strong ties between known people and places (against the society of strangers that exists mainly in the public sphere). Accordingly, the anxiety of cohesion appears as a lament of lost heritage, weak social ties, waning local commitment and disappearing cultural homogeneity. The surge of interest in recent years in social capital as the integrating resource of the plural modern society is symptomatic of this attempt to infer states of collective well-being from the quality of local associational life. The social capital narrative looks to restoring social bonds within and between communities, as it does to the active participation of citizens in civic life, judging the trust, mutuality and capability released as the catalyst of creativity and social togetherness. Its policy adoption has been ubiquitous, rolled out through programmes aiming to restore fractured neighbourhoods and build civic involvement, interpersonal and inter-cultural contact, vibrant public spaces, and community feeling in general. The aim has been to return modern society to the cares and inventions of belonging in small worlds.

If there is a keyword in nomadic thinking, it is 'cosmopolitanism'. Common to the many versions of cosmopolitanism today is an acceptance of mixity and mobility, ties with distant and different others, and care for worlds beyond the familiar and the near. Cosmopolitans consider the narrative of local community as an anachronism or constraint on those who do not conform, wish to be different, or belong to other spatial gatherings. For them, bounded communities lack the capabilities and cultural dispositions that people immersed in multiple webs of affiliation possess (Simmel, 1964); a last resort for people without access to multiple relational worlds. Their interest lies in looking for ways to work the grain of globalization – the energies of mobility and migration, global cultural exchange, transnational organization, plural affiliation – in order to sustain an ethos of care for home and the world. The bindings of universal reason, world society, internationalism and transnational democracy are seen as the building blocks of such an ethos.

The Material of Attachments

Although the geographies of affiliation traced by communitarians and cosmopolitans are different, the normative concerns are similar. Troubled by the fractures of individualism, anomie and social disconnection, both seek to restore the society of human obligations (between individuals and towards communal interests). It is hard to fault such 'peace proposals', to borrow Bruno Latour's (2004a) evaluation of Ulrich Beck's (2002) appeal for a new cosmopolitan politics to deal with the dangers of globalized risk, but a question prompted is whether the proposals must be restricted to a subjectivity of human recognition and care. As Latour asks, why must 'cosmopolitics' fall short of an interest in the cosmos itself, including 'all the vast nonhuman entities making humans act' (p. 453)? The same can be asked of communitarianism.

Any cursory glance at the composition of contemporary human attachments – in virtual space, to objects and other material entities, and in the public arena – suggests that many kinds of intimacy can flow into a politics of care. In doing so below, with the purpose of looking beyond the binary of cosmopolitanism and communitarianism, the aim is not to ignore negative feelings aroused in these spaces of everyday affiliation: the anger, terror, suspicion, delusion and betrayal that circulating images, words, things and bodies provoke, so often as the means of selecting friends and enemies, home and the outside (Runciman, 2008; Ngai, 2005; Tilly, 2005; Herzog, 2006; Turnaturi, 2007). Instead, the intention is to show that a politics of care, if this is the appropriate approach to integration in the society of strangers, can be decentred from considerations of interpersonal obligation and civic orientation which will prove to be elusive in the hyper-diverse and fluid community.

Hub-and-spoke attachments

It is a truism that growth of sophisticated communications systems linking faraway people and places has transformed the geography of social ties. Early commentary on developments such as mobile telephony or Internet-based communication treated the latter as substitutes for old forms of social interaction. Typically, the response was either nostalgia for a disappearing world of interpersonal intimacy and local commitment, or interest in the potential for relational proximity at a distance offered by new technology. New social spaces such as Internet communities or dispersed social networks were compared to old spaces of affiliation, which remained the standard of measure (e.g., of trust and mutuality). They were not viewed on their own terms. As the new communication media become absorbed into everyday life, the view grows that old and new spaces of interaction coexist, overlap and even shape each other (Wellman, 2001; Clark, 2007), supported by research showing that the ubiquity of digital networks has neither displaced interpersonal contacts nor weakened social ties.

The Pew Internet and American Life Project, which undertakes large-scale surveys of Internet use in the USA, finds, for example, that high levels of surfing (to gather information or participate in virtual communities) coincide with more people seeing each other in person and talking on the phone (Boase et. al., 2006). It also finds, importantly, that habitual usage of the new media is changing the structure of social interaction (e.g., allowing social capital to be formed through contacts and resources acquired through the Internet). Similarly, conclusions are drawn by research on the social worlds sustained by multimedia technologies. These are worlds sustained by phones and microprocessors of various kinds, combining voice, visibility, text, email, photos, music and videos, allowing, typically, teenagers and young adults, who switch effortlessly between different communication domains, to maintain contact, cultivate relationships, scan horizons, buy and sell things, participate in chat rooms, write blogs, join specialist groups and so on.

What is emerging from such research is that the nature of mediated engagement is only in part purposeful and short-lived; about maintaining ongoing connections. It is also about the everyday inhabitation of new worlds of interaction with their own ethnography of engagement with known others and strangers, and their own situated etiquettes, reciprocities and affects, spilling over into other spaces of engagement. The caricature of the hyperconnected geek living in a closed virtual world and incapable of sustaining meaningful social relationships outside of this world is just that – a caricature. As social familiarity with multimedia technologies grows, and as sophisticated software capable of integrating web, image, video, voice and sound becomes available, the case grows stronger to see virtual habitats and physical habitats as a single yet variegated space of being with others. And, as such, more is being added to the ecology of social possibility, rather than any subtraction from an old world of physical and proximate ties. It has been shown that mobile phone usage, for example, supplements physical contact and socializing, reinforces networks of care, strengthens elective affinities, enables participation in specialist networks and campaigns, and helps to forge new relationships (Chambers, 2006). As Yochai Benkler observes, the new relationships will not:

> displace the centrality of our more immediate relationships. They will, however, offer increasingly attractive supplements as we seek new and diverse ways to embed ourselves in relation to others, to gain efficacy in weaker ties, and to interpolate different social networks in combinations that provide us both stability of context and a greater degree of freedom from the hierarchical and constraining aspects of some of our social relations. (Benkler, 2006: 377)

Benkler's observations suggest that the 'web of group affiliation' today looks different from the time when Simmel coined the phrase in 1922. An old architecture of concentric social worlds that defined identities in quite strong ways – with family, rural community and tradition on the inside and urban existence and modern society on the outside – is being replaced by a hub-and-spoke architecture, radiating outwards from individuals and placing them in a variety of relational networks offering different types of ties (weak or strong, dispersed or local, temporary or stable, sparse or populated). The new architecture offers more sites of connectivity, opportunity and identity to the networked individual, with more relational possibility to those on the physical periphery or let down by traditional frames of social identification such as family, community and religion (Pescosolido and Rubin, 2000). Today, the technological lies at the centre of social capital formation, with the latter itself transformed in its yield and potential.

But even more comes into view if we consider the continuum of virtual and physical interaction not only as a communication space, but also as a space of human dwelling, with profound implications for individual and social subjectivity. Deborah Chambers (2006) claims that the rise of new spaces of interaction is not about making social ties more 'thinned out, fluid and transient' (p. 154), but about new rules of social being. She notes, for example, that as ties become more and more elective, traditional habits of attachment based on loyalty or given community are being displaced by tests of affiliation based on moral conduct, friendship and mutual care. Increasingly, it is proof of affective and ethical conduct and shared outlook that is sought (spilling over into traditional sites of affiliation such as families and communities), in the process altering the meaning of what it is to be social and caring.

This includes the role of non-humans. Commonly, the communications infrastructure – the assembly of cables, machines, screens, software, and electronic flows – has been seen as exogenous to the texture of social relations. However, hub-and-spoke networks invite consideration of the agency of all elements – material and virtual, human and non-human, visible and invisible – assembled together to form ecologies of human being and dwelling. The assemblage and its maintenance are what make these networks a 'microsociological' environment with powerful effects on subjectivity, as Karin Knorr Cetina (2005: 215) observes from her research on software-aided global financial or terrorist networks. Her work shows how habits of surfing these intricate but lightly coordinated transactional environments, with the aid of all sorts of intermediary, shape subjectivity and stance. Knowing, feeling and acting with others relies, for example, on technologies of amplification for effectiveness (e.g., powerful dissemination engines or domination of strategic user sites), texturing of the interactive space by hardware, software, screen iconography, databases and usage patterns, and tools of carriage and storage that allow multiple temporal and spatial zones to be brought into the temporal and spatial present.

For financial traders, these devices make the face-to-screen and ear-to-phone environment a social world, enabling transactions by equipping individuals to become traders with particular qualities in a virtual marketplace. Within its inhabitation, information and opportunities are sorted, trust and loyalty constructed, decisions made about who and what counts, and professional and social identities honed through habits that include objects, data, software, images and voices as co-actants (Knorr Cetina and Bruegger, 2002a). The same can be said about the agency of the networks inhabited by al-Qaeda activists, where the combinations of face-to-face, face-to-screen, downloaded files, wired dogma, phone secrecy, and other elements of a closed interactive world powerfully shape thought and practice. Knorr Cetina (2005) shows how its inhabitation orients the activists to imagine time as the passage from an unjust present to a just future through *jihad* and martyrdom, to develop a discipline of patience and preparedness based on cellular organization and network communication, and to cultivate strong feelings of power and legitimacy in a rich field of images, words, sounds and recitations that bind together a dispersed community of believers.

In the network society, it is the habit of acting in a distinctive transactional environment, and in ways that allow no easy separation of humans and non-humans or distinctive spheres of social interaction, that shapes judgement about friend and foe, home and the world, community and its other, belonging and aspiration. Divorced from the materials and rituals that give social ties their shape, meaning and content, to observe that contemporary social ties are becoming more elective, dispersed and plural than in the past is to say little definitive about whether, as a result, modern societies are becoming more or less caring, more or less civic (Castells, 2009).

Material intimacies

To recognize the materiality of the transactional environment is to consider the possibility that attachments formed with and through things (and nature for that matter) shape the nature of ties between humans. This is exactly the orientation of emerging work on material culture interested in the details of how the object world – from tools, machines, and communications infrastructures, to toys, gadgets, ornaments, prosthetics and buildings – is implicated in the human experience. Objects, and ties with them, are shown to be part and parcel of human identity, intrinsic to human feelings, including those towards strangers. 'Things', as Daniel Miller (2010: 52/3) writes, 'the whole system of things, with their internal order, make us the people we are. And they are exemplary in their humility, never really drawing attention to what we owe them. They just get on with the job.'

If, as Miller claims, 'culture comes above all from stuff' (p. 54), it makes no sense to think of the object world as a corruption of otherwise true human qualities. Such thinking has been a hallmark of sceptical writing on modernity for a very long time, linking commodity fetishism to cultures of individualism, greed and alienation, blaming reification and technological dependency for destroying cultures of craft, sociability and civic engagement, worrying about the departure from true human nature owing to artificial alterations of the body. Against these doom-laden accounts of human nature separated from itself, only siren voices have stood out, unwilling to dismiss offhand the enchantment of valued objects and technologies that make life that bit easier, happier or more exciting (Bennett, 2001).

Out of a more textured ethnography of humans and materials in relation is arising a theorization of the object-world as anything but inanimate. Things are seen to possess 'creative élan' (Bennett, 2010), to be part of the human condition, proof of the constitutive hybridity of humans and subjectivity formed and performed through enactment (Haraway, 1991; Thrift, 2005a). Here the assumption that objects enter from the outside to alter the private or public lives of humans is rejected. Instead, the entanglement of objects and humans is taken as given, the nature and intensity of human care – towards the world and one another – understood to be shaped in situated material practice. We see this most clearly in Daniel Miller's (2008) book *The Comfort of Things*, which explores people's intimacies with everyday possessions – music collections, photographs, furniture, Christmas decorations, laptops, memorabilia, ornaments and more. In Miller's hands, the intimacies turn out to be the stuff of living, giving meaning to people's lives, shaping identities, organizing memories and ongoing relationships, influencing attitudes towards neighbours, strangers and the world at large.

Miller shows how the intimacies have 'much more to do with actually constituting the people themselves rather than just standing for them' (p. 158). He does this through portraits of attachment in thirty homes on a terraced street in South London. Miller traces the cares, identities and affiliations of people through practices of home-making and affective care for possessions that are always more than things owned. The practices and objects dance into play as prosthetics of human being. The tidy apartment without many possessions speaks for, and is, George; an occupant who has always lived in care homes, held no intimate relationships, and speaks clinically about waiting in this liminal space 'for his time on earth to be over' (p. 17). The sparseness of the flat and the lack of desire to bring things into it express George in his loneliness and quiet desperation. They are not simply measures of his state of being. Further along the street, in contrast, Miller opens the door to Mr and Mrs Clarke, immersed in Christmas decorations, carefully curated rooms and thoughtfully prepared meals. Here we find an intimacy of space and a form of material care that epitomize the craft attentiveness – the skills of cultivated beauty and harmony – shown by the elderly couple for each other and their extended family.

The book abounds with insight on the vitality of objects and their role in human formation. We meet Marjorie, whose little mementos of the forty children she has fostered are a record of her family life, radiating care, whose constant alterations in her appearance speak for her desire to stay young and socially connected, and whose moral compass is expressed in the way she lives with her possessions. We meet Mrs Stone amidst the religious books, music and pictures that enrich her otherwise solitary existence and reaffirm her community ties, while the many photographs of her extended family scattered around the house remain a memento of a past life and past intimacies. We meet Dave, living alone in an all but empty flat, clinging on to a CD and photo collection that have become the ballast, witness and staging post in a life in which nothing has come easy, hazed in heroin addiction and many melted relationships.

In all these vignettes, things and relationships with them return as the stuff of social ties and affects. The entanglements make for ties with known and unknown others, always without straightforward civic and political connotations. In Miller's street, the good citizen craved by communitarians and cosmopolitans – well connected, socially motivated, non-materialistic – is a rarity. We encounter only Charles, a man of Spartan needs and strong friendships, who is a pillar of the local community, running the Neighbourhood Watch, fighting off developers, mobilizing neighbours and leading the campaign to protect local public amenities. Class, education, connectivity, biography, lifestyle and sense of place all weave into his strong sense of civic duty. None of this exists in the rest of the street, where 'most people didn't even seem to know their neighbours, and there was very little social interaction based around the street itself. This was not a place one could imagine holding street parties. Even long-term residents could only talk about local society and neighbourliness as something historical, not a feature of contemporary life' (Miller, 2008: 153).

Does this absence make the inhabitants of the street lesser citizens, socially indifferent and closed off from the world, or is such an account an invention of a discourse on social ties that neglects the affective push of material culture? More likely the latter, for Miller's research shows clearly how domestic material care bends social outlook and interest: George's frugality also revealing a numbness to bureaucratic society and an aversion to social engagement; Marjorie's and the Clarkes' curatorship of things and family extending to interest in the caring society; Mrs Stone's religious paraphernalia strengthening her ties to Britain rather more than the faded photographs of kith and kin linking her to Jamaica; and Dave's slow realization that the space and things in his council house that provide the basics of a decent life stem from an enabling welfare state.

In sum, the material of dwelling in different transactional spaces cannot remain outside explanations of social identity and affiliation. It forms the habits of negotiation of the familiar and the strange, the inside and the outside, the private and the collective. Care for the world and social positioning emerge out of these habits of inhabitation that blend perception and performance, intent and experience, and affective ties with many persons and non-humans.

Regimes of Bodily Worth

Another omission in writing on social ties is the neglect of intersections of biology and culture, of how bodily dispositions affect associational propensities. Bodily composition

– cerebral, neurological, genetic, molecular, psychological, physical, sensory and emotional – is centrally implicated in making humans into thinking and feeling beings, social subjects and cultural actors. The neurosciences and the cognitive and behavioural sciences offer considerable evidence to confirm that thinking and feeling are intertwined, that humans cognize through the senses and neurological reflex, that perception and judgement precede consciousness, that body and mind are in constant play with each other (Damasio, 2003; Johnson, 2006). Social research sensitive to these findings increasingly recognizes that stances towards others and the world – perceptions, values, beliefs and practices – are formed from the entanglement of cultural and biological biography (Connolly, 2005; Castells, 2009).

This is not the aspect of bodily sensing that I wish to explore here, partly because the connections between biology and habits of human categorization are taken up in chapter 4. Instead, I dwell briefly on the significance of state regimes of categorizing, evaluating and disciplining human bodies, that is, the biopolitics of naming and placing the normal and abnormal body. Biopolitical regimes name the bodies, traits and behaviours that count more or less in a society, laying down norms and rules of acceptability and unacceptability, mixing coercion and consent. As a raft of work pioneered by Foucault shows, biopolitics never only involves the impositions of authority, but is also sustained through everyday social conduct, precisely why it must be interrogated in any explanation of living with difference. Biopolitics is a means of 'getting close to what human beings take themselves to be' (Rose, 2007: 25).

Contemporary biomedical developments, perceived as therapies of well-being and markers of social worth, serve as a good illustration of how biopolitics and subjectivity are linked together. For those who can afford them, a raft of therapies have become available – administered professionally, over the counter and by individuals themselves – and are talked about as life necessities by health, fashion and fitness campaigners, politicians and policymakers, and the mass media. Nikolas Rose (2007) describes this as no less than a change in the meaning of personhood, involving new norms of individual and collective subjectivity based on bodily manipulation at every level (genetic, cellular, psychological, sensory, physiological, existential), and involving diverse therapies such as fitness, dieting, cosmetic surgery, organ replacements, drug enhancement, and genetic, chemical or hormonal recomposition. In this culture of treating the human body as a machine with detachable parts that can be repaired or replaced (Hacking, 2007), a new kind of subjectivity is being formed. For Rose (2008: 24–5), 'we are increasingly coming to relate to ourselves as "somatic" individuals, that is to say, as beings whose individuality is, in part at least, grounded within our fleshy, corporeal existence, and who experience, articulate, judge, and act upon ourselves in part in the language of biomedicine'.

These changes in bodily culture are not confined to how individuals see and act upon themselves. They represent the 'somatization' of politics itself. For Rose, the 'direct mapping of personhood, and its ills, upon the body or brain', supported by raised public awareness of every detail of the body and its connections with well-being, is now 'the principle target of ethical work', linking 'what we do – how we conduct ourselves – and what we are' (p. 26). Bioconduct is the measure of what it means to be a good citizen, or a responsible subject, evaluated through norms of healthy living, medical awareness and preventative care, and enabled by various curative techniques and lifestyle choices. Those who fall short by choice or circumstance – and the group includes the stranger without means or necessary cultural prerequisites – are being reconfigured as somehow deficient and deviant or unwanted citizens. The body and its parts, biomedicine, cultures of well-being and conducts of living have become measures of social worth and political subjectivity, part of the sorting machine of good and bad citizenship.

The result is a new 'ethopolitics' of community and belonging, involving 'attempts to shape the conduct of human beings by acting upon their sentiments, beliefs, and values – in short, by acting on ethics', aided by 'self-techniques by which human beings should judge and act upon themselves to make themselves better than they are' (Rose, 2007: 27). Such attempts amount to a substantial reordering of the rules of social evaluation through therapies of the self, models of personhood validated by experts, professionals and governments, incessant media commentary on the perfect body and its corruptions and biomedical necessities, and projections of the good society based on the bodily form of the individuals taking control over their lives. They rely on elective belonging and responsible living in a biologically defined social order. Accordingly, affiliation choices, judgements about others, understandings of community and standards of citizenship are derived from catalogues of vital states of being. People's eating habits, states of fitness, physical appearances, psychological states, and medical conditions, increasingly speak for their worth.

Biopolitical regimes – and there is more to them than simply the politics of the healthy body – define community, its membership and its affective qualities. Their rules of enforcement and compliance are crucial determinants of belonging, including sentiments of citizenship and affiliation, working in the background of consciousness, casually sorting out the value of different biological bodies. The ordering of the indigene and the stranger, as we shall see in the chapter on race, occurs well before and long after any declaration of commitment by the stranger or the citizen to community or to various kinds of person.

Friendship Networks and Intimate Publics

To return to human leanings, there are still other mediaries of community and fellowship. An important site of affiliative orientation today is friendship. Work on friendship, like that on material culture, tends to be less alarmist about a world of declining social ties. In following social proximities as they occur, rather than matching them against an ideal type of the good society, communitarian or cosmopolitan, such work finds friendship to be an important primer of social care and solidarity (Derrida, 1997; Pahl, 2000; Nancy, 1993). Deborah Chambers (2006), for example, claims that many contemporary forms of association – queer communities, men's and women's groups, urban social movements of various kinds, youth networks, issue-based coalitions, professional communities, virtual communities – tend to be held together by loyalties of friendship. Care and solidarity here relies on treating peers as friends, valued for what they put in, for being there in adversity, for earning respect on the basis of their actions as equals and reciprocal partners.

Chambers argues that the networks of elective affinity that proliferate in post-traditional societies, possess forms of mutuality and obligation that have been largely ignored in conservative accounts of social ties. Following Derrida (1997), she sees in these networks a new symptom of social loyalty and affinity, one that values reciprocity, and is wary of compulsions of family, tradition, nation and ideology. While general projections of friendship as the measure of empathy in the society of strangers, such as Derrida's writing on friendship and hospitality, can be criticized for underestimating the raw power of the politics of nation and nationalism, the democratic openings of elective affinities that now mediate many spaces of social engagement should not be ignored for what they say about new ways of organizing community.

This is made amply clear in Leela Ghandi's (2006) discussion of friendships struck in the most unlikely and adverse circumstances between Indians and British intellectuals and activists during the late Victorian period – friendships that drew on shared concerns, mutual respect and cosmopolitan aspiration, cutting across an entrenched politics of opposition between bloody defence of empire and fervent anti-colonial mobilization. Ghandi claims that during this unlikely period, 'multiple, secret, unacknowledged friendships and collaborations between anticolonial South Asians and marginalized anti-imperial "westerners" enmeshed within the various subcultures of late Victorian radicalism' (2006: 10) enabled a new cosmopolitanism that broke free from the unyielding nostra of conservation or reform on each side. Out of a fervent exchange of subversive ideas, a shared programme of human emancipation emerged, integrating the values and practices of vegetarianism, animal welfare, sexual equality and theosophy into socialist, libertarian and anti-imperial thinking. In this almost implausible alliance between distant strangers who ran the risk of severe persecution from their respective authorities, according to Ghandi, commitment and mutuality depended on 'friendship as the most comprehensive philosophical signifier for all those affective gestures that refuse alignment along the secure axes of filiation to seek expression outside, if not against, possessive communities of belonging' (ibid.).

The interesting claim here is that friendship allows new intimacies to be struck and sustained, new worlds to be imagined and desired, through a relational dynamic of co-cultivation, mutual regard, and affinity between unexpected allies. Friendship of this kind is plentiful today, extending also, as Fran Bartkowski (2008) has suggested, to non-humans – embryos, technological beings, animals – who have become 'kissing cousins', intimate others who talk back, require cultivation and sometimes respond affectively. Of course, there is a risk of overstating the radical qualities of friendship, which in the main cements a tryst with the already known, similar or familiar. Perhaps the point to be made is that any venture into new alliances and allegiances – including with the stranger – requires an affective link, one that can be nourished by openness to fruitful exchange with the unknown and distant.

And this occurs especially when there is a common interest or concern, binding strangers emotionally even if not personally. We see this in Lauren Berlant's (2008) study of publics formed around early twentieth-century blockbuster films and popular novels such as *Show Boat* and *Loves of a She-Devil*. In her book, Berlant does not pursue the familiar argument that these films and novels formed an imagined community that Americans came to feel part of and care for, by emotionally living out the American way of life or its core values. Instead, she explores their role as spaces of identification, as a 'porous, affective scene of identification among strangers that promises a certain sense of belonging and provides a complex of consolation, confirmation, discipline, and discussion about how to live as an *x*' (p. vii). Drawn by epic films and novels that achieved mass circulation during the early years of a forming American public sphere, millions of Americans – white women in particular – began to cohabit a shared intimate space. The dramas, intensively felt and extensively discussed, became summaries of the American story and its account of the 'true' American woman's duties and cares, hopes and aspirations, and differences from the 'other' woman at home and abroad. Stereotypes of self and other, and of past, present and future, not only sprang forth from the blockbuster, but also began to be absorbed intimately as measures of conduct, well-being and hope.

Berlant's argument is that the popular politics of America – including judgements about friend and foe or about the familiar and the strange – was sustained by the affective swirls of such intimate publics. On the basis of such evidence, Berlant concludes, more generally, that 'politics, mediated by publics, demands expressive assurance, while political subjectivity is, nonetheless, incoherent; that ideological incoherence or attachment to contradictory ethics and ways of life is not a failure but a condition of mass belonging' (p. 22). This is precisely why the tools of political persuasion have for so long worked on public sentiments, despite the rhetoric of rational preference since the Enlightenment. As Jason Frank (2005) argues, eighteenth-century moral sentimentalists felt confident in claiming that the civic subject would arise out of 'ongoing encounters with enthusiasm' taking 'precedence over the articulation of command mentality' (p. 372), stirred by 'that uncommon, extraordinary passion ascribed to those who bring the new into the world: heroes, poets, orators, musicians, even philosophers themselves' (p. 389). Similarly, in the modern age, political campaigners have worked assiduously to develop tools that can stay close to the ambivalence, incoherence and contradiction that animate intimate publics (Amin and Thrift, 2012; Hariman, 1995 and 2009a; Lazzarato, 2004; Castells, 2009). This is how some strangers and worlds come to be *felt* as anomalous, as Sianne Ngai's (2005) book *Ugly Feelings* reveals, showing how a history of caricaturing the African-American in books, films and television as excitable and susceptible has sustained a politics of nation fixed around sentiments of frustration, anxiety, paranoia and disgust towards the non-American American.

Work on social ties has largely ignored the significance of intimate publics, in the process forgetting to acknowledge the myriad gatherings (e.g., Internet communities of various kinds, cinema enthusiasts, bloggers and tweeters, newspaper and magazine readerships, television publics) in which the circulation of feeling defines community and its outside (Lazzarato, 2004; Terranova, 2007). Gabriel Tarde (1989 [1890]) understood this more than a century ago in his explanation of public culture as a swirl of contagious feelings that form the imitating crowd (see also Barry and Thrift, 2007; Borch, 2005). Contagious feelings, which spread through the collective unconscious (see chapter 3 for an urban illustration), render the commons tangible and bring the collective into the heart of personal cares and interests. They muster mass energy around stories of legacy and future travel, the community to be defended and the contaminations to be eliminated (Toscano, 2007). Intimate publics are no distraction from the 'real' substance of social life, but rather the spaces in which a dispersed population becomes energized in a political society with distinctive yearnings and leanings (Laclau, 2005).

Conclusion: Social Ties and the Politics of Integration

To recognize the many ways in which individuals become collective subjects and caring citizens is to put into context, and ultimately look beyond, a politics of human recognition to integrate the society of strangers. Public sentiments today are dispersed across many sites of affiliation. Instead of seeing them as a dissipation or distraction that must make way for communitarian or cosmopolitan attachments to ensure cohesion in the open and diverse society, might it not be more fruitful to work with them? The sentiments will not go away, and their sites have their part to play in a new politics of social solidarity and cohesion. Each site reveals something of the material and effort that goes into fashioning relational proximities and empathies, and together, the sites act as a powerful assembly of public feelings, whose juxtaposition, rubbing together and orientation towards new forms of intimacy will determine experience of the plural society as good or bad.

This is not to diminish what social transactions reveal about a social order. I am sympathetic to Charles Tilly's (2005) claim that collective cultures in a society (e.g., its propensity for violence, the treatment of immigrants, the strength of feeling for the commons) are more influenced by transactional legacies between people, and with institutions, than by behavioural characteristics (e.g., the attitudes of particular social groups) or systemic conditions (e.g., structures of economic reward or social recognition). Tilly may be right that research and policy have yet to fully grasp the power of social transactions. Where this chapter differs from Tilly's and other relational readings of the social is in recognizing non-humans – objects, symbols, technologies, intimate publics – and the multiple geographies of affiliation they support as also part of the field of social transactions, and for this, centrally implicated in the formation of collective culture. Such an understanding of social transactions opens new possibilities beyond a politics of human recognition.

In such a field of plural attachments, the worthy ambition to foster empathy between strangers through, say, local multicultural or multiethnic projects (see chapter 3) or new metaphors of collective unity (see chapter 5) is likely to flounder. Fulfilled in their given or elective communities, most people other than the very young or the already cosmopolitan are not likely to be persuaded by a politics of care for the stranger, above all at a time such as ours of detailed definition of the marked stranger (see chapters 5 and 6). This is not in any way to exonerate the self-regarding, indifferent and incurious society. This book stands for exactly the opposite but, conscious of the stubborn impediments that stand in the way of politics of care for the other, it turns to other sites of conciliation and integration, beginning with the spaces of affiliation discussed in this chapter.

A first step is to work with existing social transactions, sympathetically but critically, looking out for evidence of openness to newness and difference, curiosity for the strange and unknown, empathy for the shared and enriching commons, and commitment to a labour of cultivation. This requires suspending judgement over the greater or lesser authenticity of friendship, craft care, object love, technological society, public feelings of compassion and curiosity (Hariman, 2009b), or whether the culture of the public sphere supports consensus or vigorous disagreement (Nancy, 2000; Delanty, 2003). The stance adopted by the book towards the attentive society is one less interested in lead actors and states of being (e.g., the caring state or subject, contact among strangers, local community) than in the proliferation of everyday attentiveness as a condition of being in the world. Thus, its interest in transactional affinities relates to the potential of affective amplification, such that caring in different ways and for many things becomes central to identity and institutional practice (Tobias, 2005), steadily questioning feelings of animosity and suspicion towards the stranger as primary public sentiments (Connolly, 2008).

Affective amplification, however, as much of the rest of the book argues, will not suffice to negotiate the plural society in ways that keep harm at bay from the marked stranger. First, the many forms of institutionalized aversion and discrimination (e.g., political authoritarianism, social inequality, economic exploitation, institutional injustice) that silently neutralize positive feelings will not disappear as a result of affective amplification, even if without the latter there can be little public push for political and institutional reform. All too frequently, the very practices of care are filtered through the hegemonic institutions of social organization, altered in the process (see, for example, Povinelli, 2006, on how liberalism changed meanings of individual love in settler colonies). An expanded ethic of care will help to reign in but not neutralize the enduring sources of discrimination and harm.

Another kind of politics is also required, working on legislative change, institutional reform, principled and democratic participation, indignation against discrimination and oppression, making latent injuries matters of public campaign, and investing progressive reforms with bureaucratic power (Amin and Thrift, 2012; Žižek, 2008; Connolly, 2005; Latour and Weibel, 2005). Even an expanded politics of care cannot do without systematic and instituted organization for multiplicity and difference, equality and fairness, and common venture. What this might mean in connection with the stranger is taken up in the chapters that follow, with the next one examining the encounter between strangers in collaborative work.

– 2 –

Collaborating Strangers[1]

To be a learned ignorant in our time is to know that the epistemological diversity of the world is potentially infinite and that each way of knowing grasps it in only a very limited manner [. . .] This is the territory of the artisanship of practices, the territory of the ecology of knowledge.

Santos, 2009: 115 and 119[2]

Introduction

The modern social order, with its elaborate divisions of labour and multitude of separations (physical, cultural, emotional, dispositional), still manages to retain a good measure of transactional trust among strangers, at least those not singled out as troublesome or ill-fitting. That people remain willing to put their trust in remote actors and institutions and to cooperate with others who they do not know is a conundrum that requires explanation.

[1] This chapter reworks and develops a similar argument from an earlier article published in *Research Policy* (Amin and Roberts, 2008a).
[2] Reproduced by permission of SAGE Publications Ltd., London, Los Angeles, New Delhi, Singapore and Washington DC, from Santos, B. S., 'A non-Accidentalist West? Learned ignorance and ecology of knowledge', 26: 115, 119 (© *Theory, Culture & Society*, 2009).

Without such trust, the distributed and segmented society would break down, collapse into uncontrolled opportunism or warfare at the slightest disturbance. Attempts at explanation stretch from suggestions that humans are intrinsically cooperative and sociable (though perhaps in small collectives or under conditions of relative abundance – cf. Dunbar, 2004), to explanations rooted in the institutional history of human socialization and delegation, as Paul Seabright (2005) proposes in his book *The Company of Strangers* in connection with the endurance of cooperation:

> The answer consists of institutions – sets of rules for social behavior, some formal, many informal – that build on the instincts of the shy, murderous ape in ways that make life among strangers not only survivable but attractive, potentially even luxurious. These rules of behavior have made it possible for us to deal with strangers by persuading us, in effect, to treat them as honorary friends. Some of the institutions that make this possible have been consciously and coherently designed, but many have grown by experiment or as the by-product of attempts to achieve something quite different. [. . .] A division of labour needs to be robust against opportunism . . . participants need to be able to trust each other – especially those that they do not know. Social cooperation depends on institutions that have exactly such a property of robustness. Given the facts of human psychology, they ensure that cooperation not only happens but is reliable enough for others to be willing to take its presence for granted, at least most of the time. One such robust institution . . . is the institution of money. Another is the banking system. (pp. 4–5)

Perhaps, to elaborate on the argument of the preceding chapter, trust is not a qualified or unqualified given of human nature, nor a delegated property, but is instead a transactional good dependent upon active labour to align heterogeneous bodies. This would be to imply that the strange or different is made familiar through practices of connectivity (in all manner of space, and involving humans, non-humans and many intermediaries). Trust and collaboration in this account would be considered as relationally constituted, but not reducible to the quality of social ties, requiring deliberate organization and collective orientation. Trust in the company of strangers may be something that requires continual work.

This chapter develops this line of thinking by turning to collaborative practice, so as to identify the nature of work that sustains productive alignment between strangers. While subsequent chapters focus on other spaces of encounter, such as the public sphere or the open spaces of the city, here the interest lies in underrating how the company of strangers can become a basis for identity formation and collective creativity. The chapter turns to the organization of creative learning and innovation, in part to show that the very pulse of the knowledge economy beats from stranger proximities, assembled in ways barely recognized by both the literature on social ties and trust, and by more orthodox writing on the economics of innovation.

The chapter focuses on the prosaics of situated practice, involving learning in doing, techniques of alignment between heterogeneous bodies, and the assembly of expertise in application – in laboratories, workshops, project teams, and virtual collaborations – to explain collective creativity. Explanations of innovation as the outcome of individual genius, technological breakthrough, the production and appropriation of codified knowledge, and the integration of scarce inputs into the production function, are accordingly rejected for their failure to appreciate how the lived material practices of doing and engaging instantiate codified knowledge itself and individual expertise (Duguid, 2005).

The theorization of innovation as the yield of learning and knowing in action is by no means settled or uniform. At one end, work in science studies sensitive to the 'mangle of practice' (Pickering, 1995) from which innovations arise remains reluctant to isolate the particularities of break-through, mindful of the entanglements of mind, body and feeling, human and non-human agency, and recursive and improvised combinations that are involved in a process of always contingent and open discovery. Complementarities, frictions and serendipities, alike, of piecing together het-erogeneous materials, technologies and capabilities are considered significant, but even then, as catalytic sparks that may never come to fruition or may look quite differ-ent from original intentions. This body of work, thus, seeks to distil something from the practices of discovery (and failure), instead of looking to abstract general principles and formulae of learning and knowing in action.

At the other end, we find work that is much more certain about the social sources of innovation, and that has been avidly taken up by knowledge managers in firms and organizations. Here, learning and knowing in action are explained as the yield of particular forms of interper-sonal engagement in collaborative work, returning trust, mutuality and collaboration as the stuff of modern creative enterprise. Amidst the giant and impersonal structures of contemporary capitalism – the state, bureaucracy, con-glomerates, supply chains, codified knowledge, material and technological infrastructures, institutionalized finance – are found the simple but magical properties of small-group loyalty as the lubricant of economic creativity. What follows engages critically with this account, in agreement with the emphasis on situated collaborative practice, but, siding with the thinking on the mangle of practice, looks to delve more deeply into the ontology of learning and knowing in doing. What is uncovered is a dynamic that varies substantially between collaborative settings, is object-centred or object-mediated, and involves loyalties and obligations that are always provisional and qualified. Any link between social mutuality and creativity appears buried deep in the filigree of disparate objects, bodies and capabilities held in tension by joint work (Mitchell, 2008).

Such an examination of the detail of collaborative work is important for the politics of the stranger. The chapter shows that it is in purposeful activity that centres and peripheries are brought closer to each other, differences and divergences negotiated, and the anomalous naturalized or given productive charge. The repetitions of daily practice, the reconciliations of common endeavour, the compulsions of targets, deadlines and collective goals, and the cares and capabilities arising out of engaging work, are modes of reconciling difference. The micro-practices of creative forms of joint endeavour (remembering that many other forms, which deskill, divide, alienate and fuel animosity, have no such yield) have clear implications for strategies of social inclusion, considered at the end of the chapter, including the need to expose the contradictions of contemporary rhetoric on collaborative capitalism, which still manages to rule out certain strangers.

The Granularity of Situated Practice

'Community of practice' has emerged as a keyword in policy-oriented thinking on situated learning and knowing. It originates from the pioneering ethnographic work of Jean Lave and Etienne Wenger (1991) who, on the basis of their own involvement in boundary-spanning R&D explorations at the PARC laboratory of the Xerox Corporation during the 1980s, suggested that knowledge generation be explained as a particular kind of communal doing. They described such doing as a community of practice, formed through sustained 'relationships between people, activities, and the world; developing with time, and in relation to other tangential and overlapping communities of practice' (p. 98). These relationships were judged to be the source of creativity, based on continual enrolment and alignment of variety and difference, for example, the education of apprentices into a common venture or way of working. Wenger (1998, 2000) went on in his later writing to more precisely name the relationship between community and economic innovation, singling out three aspects of community – mutual engagement, joint enterprise and shared repertoire – as prime sources of learning and knowing; the first encouraging shared purpose and identity, the second, joint effort, and the third, the reconciliation of difference.

The power of such situated practice is further clarified by Paul Duguid (2008), another early contributor to the thinking on communities of practice. Duguid claims that in communities of shared practice and obligation, the relationship between learning *about*, learning *how*, and learning *to be*, is reinforced. Knowing emerges as a useful and tangible output of engagement, the know-how of both the individual and the group is put on display. Individuals learn to become knowledgeable partners. Shared practice strengthens and enriches the knowledge chain. It also acts as a form of ethical inculcation, gathering participants behind collective aims even when personal incentives for doing so are negligible. The spur to knowing and associating in this way is largely precognitive, for in the shared space of 'automatic, unconscious, embodied simulation routines' arises a neurological resonance, which 'allows us to harmonize other people's actions with our own and to attune our own actions with those of other people, thereby establishing empathetic understanding' (Adenzato and Garbarini, 2006: 755).

Recent years have seen an explosion of practical interest in communities of practice, with many firms and organizations looking to change their knowledge management structures (see Amin and Roberts, 2008a, for details). There has been a strong push away from top-down, technology-driven, models of innovation towards more decentred models based on collaboration between employees in dispersed groupings. In the process, subtle qualifications that only certain habituated sociologies of cooperation yield effective communities of innovation (see table 2.1) have been ignored or compromised, as knowledge

Table 2.1 Characteristics of a community of practice

- Sustained mutual relationships – harmonious or conflictual
- Shared ways of engaging in doing things together
- The rapid flow of information and propagation of innovation
- Absence of introductory preambles, as if conversations and interactions were merely the continuation of an ongoing process
- Very quick setup of a problem to be discussed
- Substantial overlap in participants' descriptions of who belongs
- Knowing what others know, what they can do, and how they can contribute to an enterprise
- Mutually defining identities
- The ability to assess the appropriateness of actions and products
- Specific tools, representations, and other artefacts
- Local lore, shared stories, inside jokes, knowing laughter
- Jargon and shortcuts to communication as well as the ease of producing new ones
- Certain styles recognized as displaying membership
- A shared discourse reflecting a certain perspective on the world

Source: Amin and Roberts (2008a: 354), compiled from Wenger (1998: 125–6)

managers reach for formulaic interpretations of the literature on communities of practice. Any original insistence on situated learning as a distinctive and hard to replicate kind of labour – for example, teaching apprentices to become masters, working with ambiguity and disagreement, sustaining particular kinds of sociality – has been forgotten (Lave, 2008). An endeavour that started by aiming to reveal the iterative, idiosyncratic and contextual nature of social learning has ended up in policy application as a lifeless caricature of social collaboration, a template for easy managerial intervention (Duguid, 2008).

The evidence itself tells a different story of learning and knowing in collaborative doing, one involving much more than human and spatial proximity and getting the mix of 'ingredients' right. It speaks of the importance of material and technological mediations, professional and reputational standards, project care and persistence, and alignment of dispersed inputs. It highlights the existence of quite distinctive ontologies of situated knowing, that vary in their patterns of social interaction, types of knowledge and innovation produced and nature of organization, as summarized in table 2.2 (and considered more fully in Amin and Roberts, 2008a). Three of the ontologies are discussed below by way of illustration.

Craft/task-based knowing

The earliest literature on communities of practice focused on task-based or craft activities, to reinstate prosaic forms of work such as photocopy repair or insurance claims processing, as well as craftwork, in the modern knowledge economy. It highlighted the centrality of community, and associated qualities such as trust, cooperation and mutual commitment, for the acquisition and application of expertise, attributing to it the power not only to bind expertise but also to harness new learning. Thus, a pioneering study by Lave and Wenger (1991), which looked at the ethnography of situated learning among Yucatec midwives, Vai and Gola tailors, naval quartermasters, meat cutters and reformed alcoholics, concluded that 'learners inevitably participate in communities of practitioners and that the mastery of knowledge and skills requires newcomers to move toward full participation in the sociocultural practices of a community' (p. 29). Inventive capability was judged to reside as much in the skills and experience of experts and overseers as in the organization of community, which allowed apprentices to learn and perform tasks, find their place in a division of labour

Table 2.2 Varieties of situated knowing

Activity	Type of knowledge	Social interaction					Organizational dynamic
		Proximity/nature of communication	Temporal aspects	Nature of social ties	Innovation		
Craft/task based (e.g, flute makers, artisans, insurance processors)	Aesthetic, kinaesthetic and embodied knowledge.	Knowledge transfer requires co-location – face-to-face communication, importance of demonstration.	Long-lived and apprenticeship-based. Developing socio-cultural institutional structures.	Interpersonal trust – mutuality through the perform-ance of shared tasks.	Customized, incremental.		Hierarchically managed. Open to new members.
Expert or high Creativity (e.g., scientists, researchers, performance artists)	Specialized and expert knowledge, including standards and codes, (including meta-codes). Exist to extend knowledge base. Temporary creative coalitions; knowledge changing rapidly.	Spatial and/or relational proximity. Communication facilitated through a combination of face-to-face and distanciated contact.	Short-lived drawing on institutional resources from a variety of expert/creative fields.	Trust based on reputation and expertise, weak social ties.	High energy, radical innovation.		Group/project managed. Open to those with a reputation in the field. Management through intermediaries and boundary objects.
Virtual (e.g, software developers, online groups, open-source communities)	Codified and tacit from codified. Exploratory and exploitative.	Social interaction mediated through technology – face-to-screen. Distanciated communication. Rich web-based anthropology.	Long and short lived. Developing through fast and asynchronous interaction.	Weak social ties; reputational trust; object orientation.	Incremental and radical.		Carefully managed by community moderators or technological sequences. Open, but self-regulating.

Source: Adapted from Amin and Roberts (2008a: 357)

and develop their creative potential within a honed collective working culture. In the integration of habits of community and collaborative work lay the authorization of expertise.

In a later study of everyday innovation on an insurance claims floor, Wenger (1998) turned to the detail of learning and improvising by community, suggesting that the mutuality, shared awareness, common repertoire, collective experience, local lore and conviviality (table 2.1), that characterized the working relationships he observed, facilitated knowledge generation in various ways over a good period of time. Such qualities hastened the rapid absorption and validation of knowledge among newcomers and they served to socialize the newcomers into a functioning division of labour and working culture. In turn, they eased the response of processors to idiosyncratic and challenging claims by giving them ready access to specialist know-how and experience, and in general fostering problem-solving through cooperation. Similarly, Julian Orr's (1996) equally influential ethnography of photocopier repair and maintenance shows that the engineer at work is never the individual expert alone, but also the member of a craft community, drawing on skills and insights generated collaboratively. Each machine with its own idiosyncrasies requires engineers to improvise, apply their kinaesthetic knowledge, recall past experiences and work imaginatively with technical manuals; all aided by regular exchange – conversations, shared stories, enactments, consultations – with other engineers and clients.

Even kinaesthetic knowing, noted to be of central importance in most writing on craft culture, is considered to be a shared good in studies of communities of practice. A notable example is Cook and Yanow's (1993) study of a flute-making workshop in which artisans with specialist skills pass on the changing product to each other, assessing the work of the previous person and returning it for further work if it 'feels' not quite right. In an environment of strong tacit sense of the quality that the final product should possess, any such decision is accepted without rancour, and in the knowledge that an adjustment can be made quickly and expertly without costly delays. There is a unity of production, customization and learning secured through the progressive tactile evaluation of the flute. Novices and master craftsmen learn to intuit, singly and as a collective, the trademark feel of the product, with the help of many arts – learnt and practised skills, the ability to feel the object with head, hand and tool, and acquired taste and judgement (Gherardi, 2009). In much the same way, Strati (1999) writes of the shared kinaesthetic knowledge of roof-tile fitters, who, needing both hands to be free, learn to develop bodily awareness through their feet, manifested in their ability to stand up while fitting tiles and to use their feet along with their hands and tools as a fine-tuned craft resource.

More could be said about the distinctions of craft knowhow, for example, the ability to draw on a practised bodily feel to make things well and imbue them with far more than use value, in the way that Richard Sennett (2008b) has done with such lucidity. However, for the purposes of comparison with other forms of situated knowing, a summary of the ecology of knowing in craft- and task-based communities of practice can be sketched from the above (recognizing that the two are not synonymous). First, the yield of codified and technical knowledge is thoroughly dependent upon its integration – through practice – with tacit knowledge and experience, embodied and (kin)aesthetic awareness, material consciousness and taste. Second, particular practices of 'community' such as shared repertoire, interpersonal ties, and close physical and affective proximities are born out of joint work. Third, although the innovative yield tends to be of an incremental nature, it remains unique and difficult to replicate owing to its distinctive aesthetic or compositional qualities, as does the knowledge perfected through everyday application and learning. Finally, the architecture of organization, for all

the collaboration and cooperation, remains centred, with
a clear hierarchy of responsibility and autonomy between
apprentices, experienced workers and 'masters'.

Epistemic knowing

What, then, of the dynamics of knowledge generation
in situations where highly qualified professionals come
together explicitly to generate innovations of a path-
breaking nature? Sometimes described as epistemic communities, these collaborations tend to be of a temporary
and exploratory nature, often among groups of scientists,
product developers, academics, artists, consultants, media
professionals or designers. They may form within organizations (e.g., product-development teams), as offsite collaborations (e.g., academics on a common scientific project)
or as networks of the 'middleground' (Grandadam, Cohendet and Simon, 2009), involving independent specialists
(e.g., media experts spread across different client networks). Such forms of 'organization by project', seeking
to foster radical newness, have proliferated in recent years
as a spread of fashion, but also due to pressure on com-
petitors in the knowledge-intensive economy to survive on
the basis of breakthrough innovations. Whether the yield
has matched expectation is an open question, with some
observers arguing that project-based creativity is often
hampered by alignment difficulties and the short duration
of collaborations (cf. Swan, Scarbrough and Newell,
2010).
    Yet there is also considerable evidence of epistemic
collaborations, bringing together experts from different
fields and organizations, successfully generating breakthrough innovations. The research suggests that, in sharp
contrast to the commonalities of culture and know-how
in craft- and task-based communities, epistemic collaborations rely on creative dissonance. Novelty comes from
fusing elements not connected before, through the

combination of heteronymous capabilities in response to a common problem or objective (Lindkvist, 2005). Experts expecting to apply their acquired knowledge to new problems frequently find themselves nudged by the frontier expectations, and the high degree of ambiguity and uncertainty of the collaborative venture, towards developing new skill and antennae (Creplet et al., 2001). This seems to emerge as a common finding in case studies despite differences in setting, purpose and morphology. 'Knowing by lurching' distinguishes search on the financial trading floor (Beunza and Stark, 2004), the collaborations of scientists attracted to renowned laboratories (Knorr Cetina, 1999; Collins, 2001), the work of corporate innovation units deliberately organized for inter-disciplinarity, the media and advertising projects that rely on cognitive distance and ambiguity (Grabher, 2004), or the staged encounters in experimental art (Yanow, 2001).

Such dissonance, however, is organized. It is structured by unorthodox rules of coordination that 'tell more than we can know' (Lindkvist, 2005: 1203); an interesting twist on Polanyi's famous dictum that tacit knowledge reveals more than we can tell. The collaborations involve experts with egos, high project expectations, tight deadlines, rudimentary rules and procedures, and considerable risk and uncertainty. The absence of interpersonal ties, fixed hierarchies and rules, and a shared working culture would threaten failure were it not for other integrating conventions. One has to do with personality. The collaborators tend to be self-assured but also motivated by inquisitiveness and an ethos of professional commitment and peer respect, which facilitates collaboration, according to Creplet et al. (2001), based on their research on business consultancy. The loyalty to the co-worker found in established communities of practice is replaced by a loyalty to a common challenge. Similarly, Grabher and Ibert (2006) note that in global advertising projects propelled by the 'canonical compulsion of freshness, mobility, and flexibility' (p. 261), traits such as professional ethic, peer recognition, calculated loyalty, and project-orientation play an important integrating role.

A second convention of integration is 'explicitation'. High-energy experimental projects facing pressing deadlines abound with scribbles, drawings, formulae, data, briefings and reports, herding collaborators towards common objects of attention, and, eventually, collective disputation or agreement. The problem at hand is made decipherable and addressed through agreed techniques of representation, analysis and resolution. Scientific collaborations would fail without such explicitation as shown by a raft of writing on the history and sociology of scientific discovery. But it plays its part also in other genres of collaboration. A study by Carlile (2002), for example, shows how shared artefacts and technologies guided a design engineering team towards a working prototype, while another one by Fischer (2001) reveals how an urban-planning project, spanning heterogeneous interests, was facilitated by an interactive electronic table that allowed people to jointly design an urban layout. Sometimes the shared concepts themselves act as bridging devices, as Kogut and Macpherson (2004) explain, to account for the global spread of Chicago School ideas on privatization enabled by the circulation of academic courses, graduates, citations, keywords and the like, in the process becoming taken-for-granted measures of worth among otherwise independent economic policy communities (see also Peck, 2010).

Third, acting as both integrating device and productive stimulus, is organized idleness. High-intensity collaborations benefit from opportunities for imaginative play, serendipity and informal interaction. They are taxing because they are short-lived, demanding, out of the ordinary and initially impersonal. Organized idleness can help to overcome these difficulties, as shown in Thompson's (2005) ethnography of a web design team, whose working culture to face challenging targets included frequent interruptions to meetings and formal agendas, many impromptu meetings and breakouts, and bursts of activity laced with seemingly idle moments. Thompson writes of a 'consciously cultivated informality' (p. 156) involving gathering around the pool table or playing with toys and puzzles in other social spaces. The structured idleness offers opportunity for rest and time for social interaction, but it also encourages improvisation and experimentation, as some corporate knowledge managers have intuited historically by pressing for expensive alterations to building and office design to encourage informal social interaction (cf. Amin and Cohendet, 2004; Thrift, 2005b; Rankin, 2010).

Finally, epistemic communities are coordinated by interactive technological intelligence. Typically, for example, new ventures in financial trading could not progress without the intelligence and integration provided by software systems, sophisticated computing and advanced communications technologies. Such tools of the trade link together co-present and distant actors into a common action space; they make up the transactional and knowledge landscape, and they enable decision-making and interpretation. They are responsible for generating the high-volume and high-speed transactional environment that demands fast thinking and interpretation, but they are also the means by which expert traders become acting subjects in a turbulent environment. New terms in the anthropology of finance, such as 'money's eyes' (Pryke, 2010), 'face-to-screen world' (Knorr Cetina and Bruegger, 2002b), 'distributed calculative capacity' (Beunza and Stark, 2004), seek precisely to capture this agency. They reveal the computer screen itself as a site of situated practice, linking traders with distant others, information sets, formulae that help interpretation, and software tools that facilitate visualization and judgement, and they capture the crucial significance of office layout, Bloomberg screens, and other tools of interaction and coordination without which no innovation or strategic decision would be possible.

If the discussion of the ecology of epistemic projects has been one sided, it is due to the crucial role of coordination devices in collaborative environments that lack a strong cultural commons. The coalitions are short-lived, the individuals self-centred, the work divided, the identities formed elsewhere and the loyalties object-oriented. Here, strangers become collaborators but not friends, co-generators of often quite extraordinary innovations, but without interpersonal ties. The tools of integration are key intermediaries: organized idleness, peer recognition, professional ethos, project interest and interactive technological intelligence. Epistemic coalitions, arguably the pulse of the knowledge economy, integrate the knowledgeable stranger in ways that are wholly neglected in communitarian writing on social cohesion.

Online knowing

The same can be said about how online communities are generally evaluated. It is often assumed that online transactions gather inputs such as information, contacts and sometimes affinities that feed into a knowledge process located offline. The online environment is not seen as a continuum of the latter or as a knowledge environment in its own right. This perception is slowly changing, partly as a result of growing research on Internet communities, some of which are recognized to be knowledge communities which are markedly different from those which depend on social familiarity and direct physical contact (Ellis, Oldridge and Vasconcelos, 2004; Johnson, 2001). This research presses for consideration of online knowledge generation as the product of a particular kind of transactional ecology, generative in its own right as a textured environment with vitality (Venn, 2010; Morley, 2006).

Clearly, not all online communities are the same. At one end of the spectrum exist large, loosely structured chat rooms, and at the other end small purposeful groups that are tightly managed. In between lie newsrooms that allow material to be read and posted but involve little interaction, online databases that permit some degree of user manipulation, clubs and game sites that involve intense interaction and emotional attachment, and online projects designed explicitly to act as learning environments. They vary in their technical, social and institutional specification, and also in their participation norms, genres of communication, conventions of interaction, and protocols of organization and management. These differences have a bearing on the knowledge-generating qualities of online communities. In many instances, conversations circulate rapidly among participants who barely know each other and who come and go at high frequency, propped up by fairly rudimentary design and data-processing facilities, and minimal attempts to control, channel and structure the conversations. The scope they offer for collective learning and knowledge generation is slight.

This is not the case with online collaborations established explicitly to broker new knowledge. Some, especially those involving participants with limited IT skills collaborating in a basic software environment, manage to sustain a surprisingly productive sociality. One example is the online site launched by professionals and lay interest groups facing similar problems that are poorly understood locally. Typically, these involve teachers or health professionals interested in improving practice respectively in the classroom or in medical practice, or patients and carers keen to learn about, and influence, health policy in specific areas of illness. The participants – pressed by the common and sometimes urgent problem – learn experimentally and iteratively in an initially 'cold' medium to forge relational affinities supporting collective learning. This is illustrated by Josefsson's (2005) study of online patient groups in Sweden, which, on occasion, have succeeded in changing medical practice by offering proposals based on the insight of carers and patients concerning symptoms, medication, coping strategies and palliative care. It is striking in Josefsson's account how the sites, mediated by an experienced web manager and a sensitive 'netiquette', succeed in sustaining a sociality characterized by humour, empathy and tact – one that opens the door to new solutions through shared discussion of sometimes highly personal experience.

There are similarities between such online and epistemic collaborations. Studies of the online communities show that factors such as the degree of participant commitment towards the endeavour, the clarity of purpose and rules of engagement, and the qualities of leadership and intermediation, are just as important for collective knowledge production and alignment (see Amin and Roberts, 2008a, for further detail). Here too, the means of enabling effective and affective communication among relative strangers with a common quest is deemed of central importance, unsurprisingly, given the absences of physical engagement. This is confirmed by Kling and Courtright's (2003) study of an interactive website in Indiana, established to find new ways of teaching science and maths. Although project developers expected a 'community of practice' to form once the technology for virtual communication was in place, success in practice was the result of subgroups being formed, aided by active and capable e-forum managers, and the development of interactive tools such as question-and-answer boxes and prompts to encourage reflection and thinking-aloud on screen.

But what of socially 'thin' online collaborations that manage to yield significant innovations? Open-source software development is an interesting example, usually attracting a large pool of technical experts initially, before settling into an exchange between the most committed participants. Typically, the ventures involve source code being released freely on the Internet, picked up by experts motivated by the challenge to solve a difficult programming problem and a desire to be recognized within a highly specialized global community. On occasion, out of a mountain of short exchanges from all quarters that mix code and half-completed sentences that disappear off screen, emerges a new software breakthrough. With all the transacting done face-to-screen, and, until recently, without the benefit of webcam or sophisticated data storage and visualization software, successful projects seemed to be those guided by shared notions of validity, sustained contribution from a core group and active coordination, usually by the project originator who directs the process of discussion and progression (Edwards, 2001; see also Mateos-Garcia and Steinmueller, 2008).

It also seems that the affective dimension is not rudimentary despite the absence of interpersonal proximities. A study of three online project collaborations, for example, shows that people participate not only because of tangible expectations such as securing the answer to a technical problem or the enhancement of their reputation, but also for intangible reasons such as the desire to meet similar minds, learn from others, work with others on a common problem and respond to a professional call (McLure-Wasko and Faraj, 2000). Such reasons explain why, even in ventures that attract free-riders attracted by the lure of a financial reward, there emerges a readiness to share valuable knowledge and to cooperate with others (as Hall and Graham, 2004, show in their study of enthusiasts attempting to crack the ten-code 'CipherChallenge' presented at the end of Simon Singh's *The Code Book*, offering a £10,000 reward). But there is more at work. The sociality of online collaboration should not be measured against an offline standard of creativity, such as trust, altruism and reciprocity. The online habitat itself is socially generative, a lived ecology structuring thought, practice, subjectivity and affect on its own terms, based on the negotiation of transactions – and other beings – through screen, software and keyboard.

Online habitats possess software systems that allow expert groups, trying to negotiate their way through complex problems, large datasets and multiple participants, the facilities of clear negotiation pathways, managed access to stored data, operability across different time spans and 'rooms' for collective reflection. Innovations such as hypermedia, interactive digital libraries, electronic memories and pop-up technologies can now support 'emergent, dynamic, exploratory interpretation' (Marshall, Shipman and McCall, 1995: 5). They help to calibrate distributed expertise, take on some of the active thinking and analysis, present a fast-moving, variegated and hidden virtual world in comprehensible ways, and become part of the human act of apprehending and interpreting. They are at once an aid to human knowing (in presenting complexities in such a way that experts can work intelligibly), part of the landscape itself through which experts must work in order to find a solution, and a second-nature prosthetic for individuals skilled at working in a virtual environment (one that taps into a honed neurology of visualization and touch). There is a tale of cognitive adaptation and ecological inhabitation to be told in explaining the knowledge practices of online experts.

The evidence concerning online creativity shows that virtual worlds can develop a social texture rich enough to support knowing by interacting with others. A commons can emerge, along with meaningful exchanges, reciprocities and affective obligations, under certain conditions of joint-purposefulness and organization. But the socialities – and the related knowledge practices and innovations – are quite different from that to be found in epistemic or craft-based collaborations. Once these collaborations are seen as the yield of – and not prior to – a distinctive ecology of practice made up of many types of actant and many modes of engagement, then the temptation to reduce collective creativity to particular forms of interpersonal behaviour recedes. Instead, new possibilities open up, such as that of humans learning to think and act in a virtual ecology with new neurological and sensory awareness and diverse material and technological intermediaries and extensions, rendering the challenge of working with distant others less a challenge of recognition than of aligning, reconciling and valorizing the many circulating ciphers and opinions (Çalişcan and Callon, 2009).

Conclusion: Knowing Strangers

The company of strangers is natural to economic creativity, a bedrock of knowledge capitalism. It is salutary to remember this at a time of suspicion or circumspection regarding the economic desirability of the stranger. With the return of economic nationalism to contest a stagnant global economy, the stranger seems required only as an invisible entity: offshore as a cheap and disposable labourer or silent consumer, and onshore as a spending but passing visitor or as a stopgap for missing skills. Every presence has to be justified, every individual accounted for and every necessity qualified as an exception. There seems little room for any relation with the stranger other than one that is exploitative and utilitarian. Yet the preceding discussion has shown that relations among strangers are natural and necessary for collective innovation; the source of new routines, processes, products and scripts in situated practice that promise real economic gain.

The question that follows, then, concerns the meaning of the phrase 'relations among strangers'. Certainly, evidence can be found to show that loyalty, trust and reciprocity are the lubricants of relationally generated knowledge, allowing strangers to draw on associational resources to act more knowingly and more assuredly (Storper, 2008). Certain kinds of collaborative work, as we have seen, rely on these properties. However, they are neither given nor the product of co-placement, but acquisitions of practice, with all its qualifications. They are studied, provisional and variable, regulated by the rhythms and routines of engagement demanded by common address and collective resolve. They are also shaped by the situation itself, and its specific modes of human enrolment. And included in these modes, as we have seen, are many material, organizational and technical devices that align and sustain the division of labour and collaborative effort. Trust, and other affiliated affects, therefore, cannot be invoked as 'as an undifferentiated explanation of coordination that black-boxes maintenance operations and socio-technical devices', as Çalişcan and Callon (2010: 21) caution. Indeed, these affects might be seen as the result of the different ways in which strangers are brought together in material practice.

By inverting the causality between learning to labour collaboratively and affective propensities, and by revealing the plural spaces and entities of human formation and attachment, the research on situated knowing stretches the meaning of 'relations among strangers' to its limit. It introduces the possibility – and potentiality – of togetherness without relational ties, of productive collective venture without strangers having to develop close affinities with each other. In high-energy epistemic collaborations and problem-oriented online explorations, but also in the craft workshop, there are other affinities and compulsions at work, from professional ethics and project deadlines to problem-orientation and material care. Here, strangers fall in behind joint endeavour and common problems, without obligation to recognize each other, disclose themselves or give up their difference and autonomy. Knowing in collaborative doing is a challenge of enrolment and alignment of the heterogeneous – human and non-human. In such doing, humans are put in place, made part of a wider unfolding, and, as a result, brought into contact with others without the necessity of recognition or reconciliation. There are so many ways in which a material culture of togetherness can be fabricated.

These observations have important implications for the political economy of integration of the stranger. Most obviously, they cast doubt on the sanity of policies to keep the stranger out or oppressed on economic grounds. This is not an argument for open migration and free handouts, for this will bring its own labour market and welfare constraints, adding pressure on settled majorities and minorities, intensifying aversion towards the stranger, and forcing newcomers into the worst kinds of jobs in the formal and informal economy. Instead, it is an argument to consider the value of dissonance, discrepancy and the unfamiliar for the knowledge economy (Callon, Mèadel and Rabeharisoa, 2002; Stark, 2009). Peripheral and plural knowledge, differentiated skills, latent capabilities, combinations of lay and expert know-how, with the surprises of the outside and of the unexpected, are the key ingredients of innovation. The stranger as one potential bearer of these possibilities is necessary for economic renewal.

However, in the economy of learning and knowing in doing, the stranger does not arrive pre-formed, nor contribute in isolation as an economic agent, but acquires potentiality through situated collaborative practice. Indeed, this is the case for all participants, as the varied examples of collaborative knowing in this chapter have shown, including old hands, known faces and distant or peripheral participants, for it is in the act of engagement that creativity is stimulated. This is why the language of attribute or measure – so much trust, social capital or cohesion, or so much supply of skills and people for the knowledge economy – makes little sense. While it may bolster new fictions of the economic cutting edge that possess considerable powers of persuasion – selling knowledge capitalism as being-in-togetherness (Thrift, 2008) or future organization as 'heterarchical' rather than hierarchical (Stark, 2009) – it does not get close to the irregular beat of practice itself. In situated knowing, success is the product of putting things together, inventing a commons, harnessing all manner of human and non-human capability, cultivating care for the task in hand, and working at the problem over and again. As Mitchell (2008: 1118) observes, 'successful calculative devices are . . . those that make it possible to conceive of a network, or market, or national economy, or whatever is being designed, and assist in the practical work of bringing it into being'.

The integration of the stranger lies in the act of collective doing, a timely reminder of the value of learning to labour together, and with craft integrity. To approach the question of social cohesion from the perspective of situated practice is to care less about who the strangers are and what they come with, than about what the collaborating participants – all strangers at the start – can achieve. It is to focus attention on the efficacy of the tools of integration, on the relational ecology itself. It is to be suspicious of the sociology of human selection, if anything for the doubt of not knowing what constitutes human potentiality:

> The object of study for sociology is not human beings but *being human*. That simple rephrasing immediately highlights the socio-technologies that are apart from our brains and bodies but are a part of our humanity. For the economic sociology of valuation there is no calculation apart from calculating devices, no judgements apart from judgment devices. Yes, we calculate, we judge, we perform. We the assemblages of humans and our non-humans perform. (Stark, 2010: 18)

If situated practice complicates the very meaning of the two letters 'we', with what confidence can the stranger be named for this or that economic outcome? The work on cultures of innovation shows that there is nothing to be gained from a politics of economic judgement that preys on the exceptionalism of the stranger.

– 3 –

Strangers in the City

Introduction

Not all forms of situated practice bring strangers into purposeful contact with each other, capable of affective transformation through engagement. The social dynamic of working, living, playing or studying together is quite different from that of strangers rubbing along (or not) in public space or sharing a cultural commons. Co-presence and collaboration are two very different things, and the meaning and affective result of situated practice in each of these sites of 'togetherness' is not the same. But this is not to say that the negotiations of co-occupancy are less significant in regulating proximities and distances between strangers, or between majorities and minorities, than those of collaboration. They are just as influential, only different, as this chapter shows, by turning to the ethnography of urban public space. There exists a rich history of claim about the behavioural and affective resonances of strangers mingling in the open spaces of a city, finding in it the pleasures or abuses of anonymity, the making of the blasé, numbed, frenzied, alienated or civic subject, the thrills or fears of crowd membership, and feelings of indifference or aversion towards the visible stranger. While interpretations have varied, the sense that the prosaics of co-presence have profound effects on what strangers make of each other has not.

This chapter turns to the meaning of mingling in urban public space. It asks whether the affects of co-presence are reducible to the immediacies of place – the dynamic of a given street or square – and to the friction of bodies, the ways in which people respond to each other. It suggests that a lot more than the proximate or the human is at work in shaping the feelings of strangers in public space, for example, the cultural influences that flow into the city through its many networks of global connection, or social habits formed out of negotiating the whole ecology of a public space, including its built form, aesthetic and symbolic feel, sensory resonances, and technological and material organization. As elsewhere in the book, the impetus to reconsider the effects of co-presence stems from an unease with contemporary policy emphasis on engineering human mingling in public space so as to resolve the antagonisms of the plural city. It is suggested that humans develop particular sensory antennae and affective dispositions – indeed become urban animals – through their experience of public space as an entanglement of bodies and things.

To elaborate, integration policies in the West for much of the post-war period tended to make light of the influence of everyday culture on negotiations of difference. They focused on national rules of assimilation and integration, the rights of the stranger, and measures to tackle prejudice and discrimination. They had little interest in the affective impulses of everyday living and interaction. Today, the situation is quite different. National and local policies have turned decidedly towards altering cultural practices to tackle the problems of social cohesion. It is unlikely that this shift is the result of raised awareness of research on situated culture, but the aim to intervene in the micro-climate of co-habitation is unambiguous. The interventions seek to either clean out the spaces of co-habitation, or engineer contact.

Turning to the former, states and publics, convinced that the multicultural policies of the late twentieth century (which accepted diversity and difference) ended up increasing cultural distance and animosity, have responded by coming down hard on minorities, youths, asylum seekers and dissenting voices, stepping up measures of surveillance, control and compliance, erecting barriers to contain or keep out those judged to pose a risk, and reigning in the boundaries of tolerance. Such interventions are guided by the belief that the only way of managing the plural society is through order and discipline, in short, the abandonment of multiculturalism. The interventions are controversial and far from convincing. Every attempt to impose order and discipline has sparked opposition, generated counter-effects, or failed to penetrate the many hidden nooks and crannies of urban life. The war on terror and fundamentalism has only served to fan dissent and defiance among those under attack, along with escalating fear, insecurity and animosity among majorities (see chapters 4 and 5). The rounding of vulnerable minorities and assimilated strangers has inflamed racism, intolerance and xenophobia and forced the injured into a feral and fearful existence. The indiscriminate use of sophisticated surveillance technologies has bred an urban culture of mistrust and punishment, pushed real criminality and harm into the shadows, and automated the means by which different sections of society are classified and evaluated. The many attempts to segregate communities in the name of urban order (in gated developments or ghettoes and through restrictions on the mobility of those considered undesirable) regularly produce backlashes that breach the walls going up.

Practitioners worried by such developments have begun to turn to more inclusive modes of social integration, looking to improve social and cultural interaction. Here, intervention has focused on desegregating schools and neighbourhoods, opening up public spaces to multiple use and diverse communities, encouraging greater contact between people from different backgrounds or enrolling them into common projects (e.g., communal gardens, sports ventures, neighbourhood regeneration schemes), fashioning reconciliation programmes to resolve disputes and animosity, and promoting an open civic culture. Cutting across local differences of approach (e.g., a greater emphasis in European cities, compared to Canadian cities, on encouraging minorities rather than majorities to participate in these initiatives) is the shared assumption that living with diversity requires interpersonal and intercultural encounter (Wood and Landry, 2007), and the intuition that urban demarcations should function as permeable boundaries and not borders that separate (Sennett, 2008a). The case for living with diversity in the multicultural city through enhanced social interaction seems more compelling and certainly wiser than the case to punish and control the stranger. But it begs one important question, namely, whether urban sociality can be reduced to the properties of the encounter.

Mingling in urban public space in the sprawling metropolis today is about people with plural affiliations (as discussed in chapter 1) passing through, carrying multiple cares, sticking to the familiar spaces, brushing past each other, bringing a host of pre-formed dispositions into the encounter. The sociality of the city dweller arises from many modes of dwelling and association (material and human) that exceed the encounter, which is precisely why work on the affects of urban encounter speaks of mixed and 'turbulent passions' (Thrift, 2005a), unpredictable feelings shaped by the detail of the situation, bodily chemistry and transferred sentiments (Wilson, 2009), and complicated personal biographies (Sardar, 2009). This is why thinking that is sensitive to such complications recommends intermediation by third parties and directed interactions to undo settled behaviour, build interdependence and catalyze positive feelings (Amin, 2002; Darling, 2009; Sandercock, 2003; Wood and Landry, 2007). But here, too, there are limits to how far the relationally constituted can be reduced to the immediate geography of contact, as Valentine (2008) notes. The cultural transactions of schools, neighbourhoods, streets or squares are never solely of that space, for the latter is a site of many intersecting relational geographies (Massey, 2005), forcing consideration of the encounter as the event of the near and remote intersecting to shape the transactional outcome, including social response to diversity and difference.

Building on earlier work (Amin, 2007 and 2008), this chapter outlines a relational and non-humanist account of the contemporary city to then reinterpret the culture of urban public space. It attempts to bring more into the transactional field of the encounter between strangers – stirrings from afar and other mediations of the local. Accordingly, it takes an interest in the urban infrastructure (layout of public spaces, physical infrastructure, public services, technological and built environment, visual and symbolic culture) and its resonance as a 'collective unconscious' working on civic feelings, including those towards the stranger. The chapter suggests that interventions in the urban infrastructure guided by principles of multiplicity and common access have an important part to play in an urban politics of living with difference. In turn, the chapter makes the case for an urbanism that is both aware of, and works through, the many spatial formations that make local collective culture. It does not see this as a challenge of making cosmopolitans out of urban inhabitants, but as one of extending awareness of how the world at large shapes local habits of encounter.

Urban Topology

With the majority of the world's population living in cities, it seems fair to argue that the human and the urban condition have become one and the same. The world is condensing into the metropolis, a distinct spatial entity. But at the same time, urban form has become extraordinarily fluid and amorphous, with the where-abouts of the city no longer self-evident. Cities have ceased to exist as bounded spaces guided by their own internal dynamics. Instead, they are relationally constituted, a space where multiple geographies of composition intersect, bringing distant worlds into the centre of urban being and projecting the placed outwards through myriad networks. The territorial city with distinctive insides and outsides has fused with the topological city defined through its relational connections.

The result is the city of plural compositional form. One form is spatial radiation, along the extensive physical and virtual communication networks that now traverse cities, situating life in a given place into daily worlds elsewhere. Spatial radiation loosens ties between co-located people and sites (Sassen, 2002; Graham, 2002), sometimes by adding another layer of linkage, sometimes through substitution as new domains of dwelling and association arise, such as the virtual community (Knorr Cetina and Bruegger, 2002a; Dodge and Kitchen, 2004). Another spatial form is urban stretch, as life in the city becomes part of the transnational corporate networks that bind together producers and consumers in far parts of the world (Dicken, 2003), or changed by the flows of money, migration, information, influence and power that circulate the modern world in organized ways (Harris, 2002; Sparke, 2005). A third, and related, compositional form is urban globality: the lived everyday formed in diasporic space – ethnic, religious, consumerist, ideological – and through participation in transnational social movements and media cultures (Pieterse, 2003).

The contemporary cartography of the city is porous, distended, and zygotic, as the distant and the proximate, the virtual and the material, the present and absent, the passing and the settled, merge into a single existential plane (Farías and Bender, 2010). The dynamics of location – happenings in a place on the map – are ordered by the play between multiple spatial orders of being and becoming (Olsson, 2007). Both the cosmopolitan city and the most remote of places are becoming intersections of rhythms formed in diverse spatial envelopes, demanding to be considered as spaces of 'throwntogetherness' (Massey, 2005). This includes the formations of public culture, for, in the city of multiple provenances, different groups – from settled and segregated communities to mobile migrants and professionals – press to be understood in their multiple affiliations, frictions of co-presence and variegated response to the contingencies of thrown-togetherness. Thus, strangers are not of necessity tied to each other or inclined to recognize each other, dispersed as they are throughout the city, familiar with only particular spaces, locked into elective networks of belonging and intimacy, frequently compelled to stave off difference to cope with the multiple assaults of urban modernity (as originally suggested by Simmel, 1971). In public space, strangers can play out their differences, inhabiting many networks of communication and affiliation while on the move (from global fashion worlds and cultural fantasies to familiar faces and voices at the end of mobile phones).

Yet these freedoms of topology are also constrained by the regulatory machinery of a city. Every public space comes with its distinctive rules of orientation, enshrined in principles and acts of public organization and order that, in signalling clear cartographies of permissibility and possibility, fix the terms of engagement between different subjects in the public arena. Typically, the decisions of urban elites and planners in a given city shape the chances of different social groups and their position in the social hierarchy, through the specifics of land use allocation, social and cultural policy, economic strategy, housing distribution, governance of public space, access to collective services, and symbolic projection of the city. The multiplicities of urban flow and excess are regulated by these silent fixes of urban order, allowing more breathing space to the stranger in one site, but less in another (Lancione, 2011).

Urban Sentiments

The silent fixes are also implicated in the formation of urban sentiments. The urban morphology – a city's layout, material form, infrastructure, technological qualities, regulatory environment, natural and symbolic landscape – can be seen as the experiential field in which collective feelings towards specific sites and the city as a whole, along with judgements of co-presence, arise. It is the field in which reflexes of urban living, including relations among strangers, are formed without conscious thought and deliberation. These reflexes, as the discussion below on public space illustrates, arise out of the entanglement of urban morphology and human experience, the negotiation of the city as an assembly of humans, things, symbols, technologies, matter and nature. To acknowledge this is to accept that urban feelings may be shaped by the body's receptivity to all that fills a space, from its machinery of organization and orientation, to its atmosphere charged by smells, light, bodies, buildings, objects, signs and a lot more.

A body of writing in social theory has grown showing how non-humans are implicated in human being and becoming (Latour and Weibel, 2005; Bennett, 2010; Gregson, 2009; Ingold, 2006; Rose, 2007; Miller, 2008; Pickering, 2010). So too has thinking on the involvement of matter, nature and technology in urban social life (Graham and Marvin, 2001; Amin and Thrift, 2002; Pile, 2005; Latham and McCormack, 2004; Swyngedouw, 2004; Castree, 2005; Gandy, 2005; Marvin and Medd, 2006; Hinchliffe and Whatmore, 2006; Heynen, Kaïka and Swyngedouw, 2006; McFarlane, 2011). The work on urban material culture shows, for example, how the everyday machinery of urban circulation, involving timetables, software systems, communications infrastructures, data classification tools, architectural designs, and an array of objects and machines, underwrites urban survival and recovery, affects the life chances of different social groups, and makes humans behave in certain ways towards the urban commons and each other. Whether this kind of melding of the technological and human is best described as 'cyborg urbanism' (Gandy, 2005) or 'machinic urbanism' (Amin and Thrift, 2002), what these terms seek to grasp is the vitalism of the seemingly inanimate urban infrastructure. They re-propose a city's transport network grid, or emergency services, or architectural structure, as an assembly of objects-in-relation replete with 'interactional intelligence' built into code, thinking machines, software systems, and human effort, and functioning under the radar and out of sight as an 'urban technological unconscious' (Thrift, 2005a). The urban infrastructure – with its own systems of intelligence – pieces the city together but also authorizes possibility, including social choice and orientation. It joins up and monitors the urban landscape, simultaneously allocating resource and opportunity, designating the spaces, activities and people that count (e.g., by selecting zones for investment and groups deemed undeserving), and establishing the rules and tempos of urban participation. Working silently in the background, the centrality of the urban infrastructure becomes all too apparent when there is a severe malfunction (e.g., when a city is brought to a halt by an energy blackout or environmental catastrophe).

The silent work also regulates the affects of living with difference. Everyday uses of public services and utilities, movements through neighbourhoods and public spaces, encounters with transit systems and technologies of surveillance, are experiences of the urban commons – more accurately habits of dwelling in the urban infrastructure – laden with affective response (Latham and McCormack, 2004). The satisfactions and frustrations of negotiating the urban commons are subliminal judgements about co-presence (see Brand, 2009, for an account of how the aesthetic of the urban landscape in Belfast has reinforced sectarianism). Achille Mbembe (2008: 38) has suggested that the urban unconscious, and its 'aesthetics of surfaces and quantities', can be thought of as a field of affective excess, able to 'hypnotize, overexcite or paralyze the senses'. Urban form itself generates distinctive public feelings: desires stimulated by the visual landscape, anxieties and satisfactions kindled by the quality of public service or protection, and angers stoked by the hidden rules of supply and allocation.

These affective accumulations give a city its particular cultural feel, including reflexes of social judgement. The sentiments formed in the urban unconscious become a tool of differentiation and discrimination between minorities and majorities, citizens and non-citizens, social classes and communities. They shape, in advance of thought and will, judgements of entitlement and blame, quick-fire evaluation in public space of who is entitled to the urban commons. The qualities of the urban unconscious and feelings towards strangers are closely interwoven. Thus, it is hardly surprising that in cities with well-functioning urban services (from comprehensive welfare and decent public services to strong minority rights and accessible public spaces), public feelings towards immigrants and migrants only too often crystallize around their claims over an urban commons that majorities consider as theirs. When publics perceive urban services, utilities and common spaces to be strained or dysfunctional, the stranger frequently gets the blame, accused of being over-demanding or undeserving. It is the personification of sentiments formed through the urban unconscious that allows this kind of association to spring into the public mind, in turn conditioning intersubjective affinities.

In cities without a shared or functioning public infrastructure (e.g., segregated cities or those with a threadbare infrastructure), the sentiments of the urban unconscious discriminate in a different way. In the segregated city, these sentiments gather around the architecture of impermeable division – the high walls, tight systems of surveillance, myths of cultural incompatibility, and rigid hierarchies of social classification that naturalize separation as the culture of living with difference. Social and spatial demarcation becomes the rule of urban maintenance, the flashpoint of opposition, the spark to imagining another urban culture, each propelled by sentiments born out of the experience of negotiating urban separation, each clear about the offending and deserving subjects. In the 'threadbare' city, collective sentiments form around the basics of urban provision, guiding judgement over the practices and claims of those deemed undeserving. In the city of mass poverty and deprivation, where formal citizenship rights bring few privileges and where nationals and immigrants constantly on the move feel little loyalty to their place of temporary or miserable sojourn (Landau, 2010), the tensions of living with difference often gather around the infrastructures that regulate access to credit, medical care, energy, shelter, water, safety, sanitation, food, transport and work (Stienen, 2009). For example, how particular social and ethnic groups, criminal gangs, moneylenders, vigilantes, and formal and informal organizations manage the distribution of scarcity forms the lightning rod of collective sentiment and inter-communal conflict (Simone, 2008, 2010; Tulchin, 2010; Roy, 2009).

Strangers in Urban Public Space

A rematerialized urban sociology introduces new elements into the making of cultures of co-presence, and with this, the possibility of a more-than-human politics of living with difference. A city's streets, parks, squares and other shared spaces have long been seen as sites of civic and political possibility by urban leaders and visionaries. The history of urban planning is one of the attempts to manage public space in ways that build sociality and civic engagement out of the encounter between strangers. This history draws on a long lineage of thought spanning classical Greek philosophy, accounts of urban modernity by thinkers such as Benjamin, Simmel, Mumford, Lefebvre and Jacobs, and many contemporary visions of the good city nostalgic about past forms of mingling. It is a history of claiming that the free and unfettered circulation of humans in open and well-managed public space encourages forbearance towards others, pleasure in the urban experience, respect for the shared commons, and an interest in civic and political life.

In modern times, such thinking has inspired the 'city beautiful' and 'garden cities' movement, and, most recently, a 'new urbanism' commending a return to compact housing, front porches, pedestrian areas, shared urban assets, mixed communities and the city of many public spaces. While the primary aim is to promote urban sociality and civic life, there lingers also the hope that vibrant and inclusive urban public spaces can act as a formative political site in an age of remote and bureaucratized politics. The busy square or town hall meeting is seen as the site of participatory politics, where claims are staked, political skills are learnt, interests are debated, collective allegiances are formed, and counterweighting to the closures of formal politics may be built.

In an age of urban sprawl, multiple usage of public space and proliferation of the sites of political and cultural expression, it seems odd to expect public spaces to fulfil their traditional role as spaces of civic inculcation and political participation. We are far removed from the times when a city's central public spaces were a prime cultural and political site. Today, the sites of civic and political formation are plural and distributed. Civic practices – and public culture in general – are shaped in circuits of flow and association that are not reducible to the urban (e.g., books, magazines, television, music, national curricula, transnational associations), let alone to particular places of encounter within the city. Similarly, the sites of political formation have proliferated, and include the micro-politics of work, school, community and neighbourhood, and the workings of states, constitutions, assemblies, political parties and social movements. Urban public spaces are arguably secondary sites of civic and political formation.

If co-presence generates civic and political resonance, it is probably in subliminal ways, through habits of negotiating shared space. But if this is the case, following the preceding discussion, the full weight of the ensemble of things, bodies, technologies, sounds, visual clues, buildings and more in public space must be considered as an atmospheric force working on civilities and incivilities, or indifferences and cares. Extending the work of early pluralists such as William James (2003), and of contemporary thinkers attentive to the dynamics and demands of complex social systems (e.g., Connolly, 2005; DeLanda, 2006), it might be suggested that human affinities formed in urban public space are responses to 'staged' multiplicity. The pluralism and vitality of an open space of gathering, its functional and symbolic order, its material arrangements, its many temporalities and spatial flows, and its proliferations of variety, trace a distinctive ecology of presence, one that is full of the surprises and novelties of unplanned interaction between disparate bodies and things, but also made legible and stable by the repetitions of habit and the rules and regulations of order and orientation.

Streets, squares and markets are simultaneously spaces of ordered interaction guided by rules of public behaviour, traffic flow, spatial planning, security and the like, and spaces of juxtaposition and friction that unsettle the known and the expected. In the balance are shaped practices of orientation, but also expectations from the space of co-presence and its diverse constituents (Degen, Rose and Basdas, 2010). This is why neglected public spaces with rudimentary or exclusionary rules of regulation breed social pathologies of anxiety and avoidance, or intolerance and harm, as subjects pass through it distrustful of the surprises of multiplicity, guided by reflexes of rejection and withdrawal to cope with the unanticipated and unknown.

In contrast, in public spaces structured for free but fair play, plural but safe flow, and controlled variety, the mingling of strangers is guided by different resonances of situated multiplicity, different kinds of social reflex. One of

the resonances of the busy street, frequented by the many
and open to changing uses and occupants, may be described
as controlled plenitude, sensed by subjects as being in a
space of possibility, but shared with others, and belonging
to none. This resonance may better explain Simmel's claim
that the free mingling of strangers in the modern city generates feelings of carefree indifference or awe and curiosity.
Perhaps, in this mingling, strangers are less mindful of each
other or of the swirls of the crowd, and more guided by a
form of sensory awareness of the space as a whole, the
reception of the entanglement of bodies, matter, flows,
atmospheres, things and design as a provisioning and enabling 'cinematic' whole (Shapiro, 2010).

By and large this sense of the cinematic whole is controlled. Humans in the busiest and noisiest spaces tend to move
and behave in an orderly and predictable fashion, unruffled
by the excesses and surprises of situated multiplicity. This is
because a second resonance of the busy public space is its
domestication by many formal and informal rhythms of
territorialization. Public spaces are a patterned ground,
with human movement and judgement steered by habit,
purposeful intent, and the instructions of assembled technologies, rules, signs and symbols. These rhythms of domestication present the potentially overwhelming as a map of
the familiar and manageable, of the unpredictable and dangerous kept at bay. But these rhythms are an unsettled resonance, and sensed as such, for they are continually tested by
the many emergent combinations that arise in a plural
space. Jane Jacobs (1961) famously celebrated urban public
spaces open to the surprises of multiplicity, the unexpected
encounter and the chance discovery. It might be added that
the possibility of newness always hovers in public spaces,
giving them their edgy feel that some value and others fear,
but always demanding from those who pass through an
ability to respond to the unexpected.

Another resonance can be mentioned, namely, symbolic
inculcation. The iconography of place, shaped by the
architecture and design of the built environment, the pro-

jections of advertising and other forms of visual enticement, and daily patterns of usage and gathering, is integral
to public being and positioning. Indeed, in the history of
writing on public culture, the semiotics of public space has
been read as the symptom of the urban, and sometimes
human, condition. An illustrious body of work, from that
of Benjamin and Freud to that of Baudrillard and Jacobs,
has sought to summarize modernity from the symbols of
urban public space that speak of progress, decadence,
hedonism, alienation or wonder (Amin with Thrift, 2007).
The displays of collective life in public spaces – from the
design of buildings and the layout of streets to monuments
that commemorate the past and advertising that projects
the desired future – play to this canon, fusing the extraordinary and the ordinary in the lived experience of space,
adding all manner of meaning to being in the company of
strangers.

Such resonances of situated multiplicity, always specific
to a given ecology of urban co-presence, influence human
behaviour in quite profound ways by stimulating particular social reflexes of adaptation. The swirls of multiplicity,
the rhythms of territorialization, the regulation of surprise,
and the aesthetics of space all temper public feelings by
working on the senses in a silent way. Awareness of this
agency suggests the necessity of a different approach to
public space as the ground of conviviality, one that must
acknowledge the limits to human recognition in the city's
streets, malls, libraries, parks and buses. It points, for
example, to interventions that attend to the resonances of
multiplicity, its compliances and compromises, and its
ominous tendencies (such as the uncontrolled crowd colonized by the powerful and menacing). Formally, this might
mean acting to protect the space of vulnerable groups so
that a sensibility of equal access grows and, informally, it
might mean reinforcing the vernacular of plural watchfulness typical of the busy bazaar, with its many 'eyes of
the street' (Jacobs, 1961), accommodations, and multiple
transactional arrangements (Simone, 2010).

Additionally, but with a different slant on the history of aesthetic intervention, the politics of living with difference might turn to the symbolic persuasions of public space. Modernist planning was an experiment of this sort, looking to monumental art, grid structures and public buildings to foster new forms of urban being by fostering affects of awe, gratitude or fear. Similarly, the history of mass congregation in public space, moved by the spectacle of numbers, moving speeches, imposing architecture, with a strong sense of place, has shown how a 'people' can be formed to unseat or maintain power. The kind of aesthetic suggested by the foregoing discussion, however, is very different. It might be called an aesthetic in the minor key, one that projects – with the help of various kinds of public art or symbolic gesture – the commons as plural, a temporary borrowing, unalienable. Typically, it seeks to not forget past injuries caused by exclusionary urbanism, such as the violence of racism and segregation, through commemorative art, or it finds ways of re-presenting public space as the domain of multicultural or experimental presence.

These kinds of intervention focus on the conviviality of the situation. Contemporary urban policy interest in conviviality, responding to work on living with difference through everyday interaction (Gilroy, 2004; Amin, 2002; Sandercock, 2003; Keith, 2005), focuses on building ties between strangers in neighbourhoods, schools, housing estates and other public spaces. In contrast, the interventions here speak to the principle of *convivium* or living together without the necessity of recognition.

Living Together

If the above interpretation of urban public space forecloses a certain politics of the stranger, it does not underestimate the potentiality of common yield from co-presence. It takes interest, for example, in interventions across the urban spectrum – from public spaces and the local media to welfare services and the public infrastructure – that might yield a culture of the urban unconscious that diminishes public interest in difference, that supports a habit of seeing the strange as familiar. F. G. Bailey (1996) has referred to this kind of collective unconscious as a civility of indifference, a skill of co-habitation without rancour, open on occasion to acknowledgement that 'bringing differences into some kind of relationship produces unforeseen capacities and experiences that are valuable – valuable because they extend what we think is possible' (Simone, 2010: 61). A deliberate attempt to foster this kind of orientation – and more generally a politics of living together without strong expectations of mutual empathy – might consider two organizing principles: multiplicity as the defining urban norm, and co-presence as being on common ground.

Multiplicity

Henri Lefebvre (1996) famously defended the right to the city as the right of all its inhabitants to shape urban life and to benefit from it. He saw this very much as a participatory right, extending beyond the conferral of entitlements of citizenship or residence. In many parts of the world, however, the denial of basic entitlements – for example, the right of migrants, minorities, and the urban poor in general to have access to the minima of survival such as food, education, shelter and hygiene – remains a major obstacle to the right to participate. Those without basic entitlements can make no claim on the city, absorbed as they are by the task of surviving against the odds, often classified as unwanted subjects. Until their right of access to the means of life is recognized as a legal or civic right, there can be no possibility of their active participation in urban life. Such extremes of denial give majorities, elites, decision-makers and the righteous reason to assume that the suppression of the wretched and the foreign is legitimate, perhaps even necessary in preserving 'community' (Appadurai, 2006).

The conferral of universal rights as a first step in recognizing urban multiplicity is far from straightforward, for it immediately raises questions about their protection and violation, and the relative entitlements of new arrivals and settled inhabitants. Neglecting these questions can only intensify social stress and division, as well as erode confidence in a city's systems of public provision. Yet the denial of rights to those without means and of means to those with rights makes little sense in a world in which intense global connectivity and flow alter the composition (and expectations) of the urban population on a daily basis. In these circumstances, the assumption that particular sections of the population possess a natural right to the city is divisive, an impediment to the principle that all those who inhabit it – from long-term citizens and established elites to newly arrived migrants and low-income residents – start out from the same position in their right to belong (Subirós, 2011). Such a change would allow urban rights to be linked to social contribution, which, depending on the means and capabilities of individuals, could take a variety of forms, from fiscal and philanthropic donations to contributions in kind or community service, so that access to rights becomes a way of building solidarity in the plural city (Fincher and Iveson, 2008).

A focus on rights, however, does not address other negations of the principle of urban multiplicity, from conscious abuses of power by those claiming authority, to the hidden injuries of class, race and gender. Generally, these abuses and injuries are worked into the discriminations of the urban technological machinery. For example, in the clockwork city, sophisticated software systems used by firms, public authorities, or insurance and security agencies, routinely affect the standing of different social subjects; sharing data from hidden cameras, consumer records, police files, ratings agencies, private and public organizations, to codify people as insiders or outsiders, dangerous or safe, worthy or unworthy. In the city of rudimentary technological systems, a different architecture of classification does the same kind of work, perhaps in a less hidden, less automatic fashion, relying on spatial segregation, direct forms of policing, and elaborate practices of racial, class and gender tagging. While one type of technological order discriminates silently and the other more visibly, common to both is the fusion of codes and conventions that simultaneously keep cities maintained and repaired as well as governed as a social hierarchy. The intelligence nested, for example, in software systems that integrate the plural spaces and times of the city, keeps urban life going in its parts and as a whole, but also permeates the systems of social selection and control. The distinction between collective protection and social discrimination is blurred, precisely why the injuries suffered by some subjects are perceived as integral to the maintenance of the orderly.

A politics of the stranger cannot ignore the ambiguities of the urban technological infrastructure. It has to find a way of ensuring that the regime of maintenance and repair sees to the cares and needs of those without voice, power or means, and that the regime of order and discipline protects the gains made. Achieving this is by no means straightforward given the hidden dispersions of the means of order and discipline. However, a first step would be to make the urban infrastructure an object of political scrutiny, revealing, for example, the selection and separation done by 'values, opinions and rhetoric . . . frozen into code' (Bowker and Leigh Star, 1999: 35). This requires a campaign to expose, ridicule and neutralize the uses of technology as a weapon of discrimination, to enforce public audit of the machinery of human categorization and selection in the city, to experiment with preventative and precautionary forms of order, and to bring the machinery of urban order under democratic control (Graham, 2010). It requires building public desire for a machinery of urban maintenance and repair that minimizes insecurity and disruption by underwriting all forms of urban life; a network of public utilities, services, institutions, spaces and transit systems understood as a commons that keeps the city on the move, acts as a life support and opportunity field, ensuring that basic needs are met.

Common ground

In the rights-based society, condescension and resentment hover close to the surface, with elites and majorities often taking it for granted that it is their business to confer rights to immigrants and minorities, held to be different, inferior and supplicant (Hage, 1998; Brown, 2006; Noble, 2009a). For multiplicity to mean more than diversity placed in hierarchical order, the commons has to be widely understood as a gathering of equals, a meeting ground and shared turf. Such an understanding may grow out of habits of daily encounter between strangers, but it also requires acceptance of a commons valued as irreducibly plural and provisioning. This chapter has argued that the many local separations, dispersed geographies of attachment and qualified proximities between strangers that characterize modern urban living make it difficult to build urban commons based on care for the other. However, an ethos of the urban as a shared plenitude might hold more promise, advanced through a culture of active usage of the city's shared resources and spaces, vigorous occupancy of the public sphere and public stewardship of the urban commons.

In the city of multiple interests and attachments, an ethos of the common ground is unlikely to arise without active cultivation, beginning with the explicit commitment of civic leaders to the shared plural city, backed by effective action against xenophobia, intolerance, inequality, injustice and erosion of the public sphere. The city that defends all those provisions required by its inhabitants – mixed and public housing under pressure to gentrify or segregate; collective services under pressure to be more selective; the vulnerable, disadvantaged and threatened under pressure to invest for the economically privileged and the rich; open and inclusive public spaces under pressure to privatize or control entry; multiculturalism and hospitality under pressure to eject and discipline the stranger; a green and diverse urban landscape under pressure to exploit commercial opportunity – demonstrates its awareness of the value of such communal life. It asks its inhabitants and institutions to act in a certain way, presenting togetherness as an opportunity for collective well-being and new formative experience, and warning those who expect the city to serve partial or privileged interests to reconsider.

But such asking has to chime with habituated experience of the city as a commons, the continual play between explication and practice, between prosaic usage of the urban commons and public articulation of what this adds to personal and collective life. It must be accompanied by systematic proliferation of the sites of shared living through which a dispersed sense of the plural communal can emerge. These sites are prosaic and well known. They include the associations, clubs, meeting places, friendship networks, workplaces and spaces of learning that fill cities, where habits of being with others and in a common space and stances towards the city and the world at large take shape. They include the physical spaces – streets, retail spaces, libraries, parks, buildings – in which being with other humans and non-humans shapes sensibilities towards the urban commons, unknown strangers and multiplicity. They include the public services, infrastructure and collective institutions, where attitudes and expectations related to the city as a collective resource, provisioning system and source of welfare are formed. They include the city's public sphere – symbolic, cultural, discursive and political – in which collective opinions and affects of community and its constituents circulate.

Across these spaces, the task for a politics of togetherness is to make the connections and dependencies visible, to reveal the value of a shared and functioning commons, to show how life chances depend upon an urban infrastructure capable of accommodating new demands and new claimants, to argue the necessity of an open and dissenting urban public sphere, to show that to damage the commons is to damage the self and future possibility. The kinds of intervention necessary hold few surprises, and include ensuring decent public infrastructure, welfare equity and 'participative parity' (Fraser, 2005: 87), vibrant public spaces, a democratic public culture and popular stewardship of the city's public assets. The greater challenge is to maintain momentum, so that care for the urban commons – and indifference towards the social status of its occupants – spreads across the social fabric, periodically reinforced by the symbolic force of various forms of urban narrative, from film and art to media propaganda and folklore. These narratives muster collective concerns and intimacies, including those related to the state of the urban commons (Stewart, 2007).

Through continual acts of renewal of the living urban commons, the city of the stranger can be built without the need to wait for a 'surplus common' to be released from the clutches of 'capital' or other imposed values of coexistence. The plural city continually undermines the clinical distinction that the 'qualitative difference between the commons and capital understood as the regime of value consists of this other surplus, which for lack of a better term, I would like to call *surplus common*. Revolutionary becoming is living the common as surplus' (Cesarino, 2008: 22). The labour 'to institute and manage a world of common wealth, focusing on and expanding our capacities for collective production and self-government' (Hardt and Negri, 2009: xiii) can begin without waiting for a time of clearance when the commons can be freed from capital and returned to collective production and self-government.

Conclusion

In its scepticism of an urban politics of recognition, the intention of this chapter has not been to devalue effort to build bridges between divided or separated communities.

On the contrary, it can only help to learn from conflict-resolution techniques honed in fractured cities such as Sarajevo, Beirut or Belfast to tackle deep-seated fears and aversions between communities (Bollens, 2007), to gather people from different backgrounds around common ventures to bridge social and cultural distance (Amin, 2002), and to work on manners of cohabitation (Wise, 2005 and 2010; Noble, 2009b). Instead, the chapter's ambivalence stems from the view that many other everyday influences shape habits of living with difference, and that being in the world involves a host of relational affinities that substitute or surround the direct encounter. Feelings formed in many other relational spaces invade the encounter, mediating the labour of inter-culture and recognition among proximate strangers, and the physical encounter is no longer the sole or privileged space of relational contact. The encounter is always mediated.

The complications of the encounter are taken up in the next chapter, by focusing on the phenomenology of contemporary racial judgement. The chapter examines the many provenances of judgement that invade the racialized encounter, making particular faces on the screen, and bodies encountered on the street, appear as threatening and impure. In seeing the body as a site of pre-formed and performed affects that are formed in a variety of relational spaces, the chapter reveals the encounter between strangers as both of the moment and therefore open to possibility (in the way desired by a politics of recognition) and laden with influences from elsewhere which require different forms of address.

The implication is that a politics of the stranger requires a crowd of breathable spaces. This goes for the city too, which cannot act without seeing itself as part of a wider public culture which imagines community as open and heterogeneous; ready for the convivial or disjunctive combinations of everyday encounter (Gilroy, 2004; Chambers, 2001), attentive to the global connections that make up a social order (Sardar, 2009) and interested in the full detail of the democratic process (Connolly, 2005). The progressive city has to establish a way of finding ventilation from other breathable spaces named in the rest of the book: new metaphors of belonging (e.g., solidarity, common life, shared concerns), exposure of the cruelties and absurdities of the vindictive present, revulsion against discrimination and prejudice, extension of the social state, and intimate publics and public spheres in which the domestic and foreign merge, and curiosity and engagement become the necessary skills to face an uncertain and turbulent future.

– 4 –

Remainders of Race[1]

The formula of revolutionary solidarity is not 'let us tolerate our differences', it is not a pact of civilisations, but a pact of struggles which cut across civilisations, a pact between what, in each civilisation, undermines its identity from within, fights against its oppressive kernel. What unites us is the same struggle.

Žižek, 2008: 133[2]

[1] This chapter reproduces an article published recently in *Theory, Culture and Society* (Amin, 2010). Since it was originally conceived for this book, and indeed as its centrepiece, it has not been revised. The article attracted four critical responses by Denise da Silva, Ali Rattansi, AbdouMaliq Simone and Couze Venn, published in January 2011, accompanied by a response from me in interview form on the journal's blogspot. The discussion focused on the biological and cultural foundations of racial legacies, the cultural and institutional scripting of community and its outsiders, the historical nature of the 'race argument', and the transgressions of racial stereotypes in everyday urban life. Given the integrity of the journal debate, and since I did not feel further changes were necessary in the context of this book and arguments developed in other chapters, I have kept true to the original piece.
[2] Reproduced by permission of Profile Books, from Slavoj Žižek (2008), *Violence*, Profile Books, London: 133.

Introduction

In 2007, I had the opportunity to visit an extraordinary exhibition at the Centre for Contemporary Culture in Barcelona (CCCB, 2007), unmasking the machinery of race. The exhibition covered the 200-year history of racial violence in South Africa perfected by the apartheid system. Using a rich mixture of text, film, photography, installations, paintings and sculpture, the exhibition told three stories. The first was that of classification, showing how the maintenance of racial hierarchy and racist violence depended on an elaborate machinery involving eugenic science, scripture, travel journals, museum displays, measuring instruments, photographs, laws, and more, to delineate the contours of community and community membership. The exhibition laid bare the architecture of racial formation and the heinous work done by it. Second, it told the story of resistance: of how the inventions of counter-classification, art, music, faith, solidarity, organization and subversion chipped away at the established order, exposing and eventually dismantling a perfected machinery of racial oppression. Third, the exhibition told the story of continuity: of how the optimism and hope unleashed after the collapse of the apartheid state, have been muted by new forms of racial oppression linked to economic liberalism and the persistence of old discriminations. The same people are stuck at the bottom of the pile despite their acquisition of new rights and freedoms.

The exhibition made me think about the archaeology of race – the play between continuity and change and between visibility and invisibility – and its role in mediating relations between racialized strangers in a given present. It made me want to look into the historical dynamic of race to better understand the scope of anti-racist action, for while the exhibition gave testimony to the possibility of change even in the most ingrained regimes of racial oppression, it also pressed home the power of institutional and vernacular legacies of race to act like a call to order, to shut down hope. In the exhibition's coverage of daily life in South Africa after the end of apartheid, echoed the familiar lament of persistence often heard in historical novels on race and from genealogists of race such as du Bois, Fanon, Said, Baldwin, Gilroy, West and Pred. The refrain of hope held back chimed with Howard Winant's (2006: 987) rueful comment, 'the age of empire is over; apartheid and Jim Crow have been ended; and a significant consensus exists among scientists (natural and social), and humanists as well, that the concept of race lacks an objective basis. Yet the concept persists, as idea, as practice, as identity, and as social structure. Racism perseveres in these same ways.'[3]

Even the most discredited ideas of race seem to return in some shape or form, as the case of biological racism shows. Today, most justifications of race rely on cultural, rather than biological, arguments, asserting cultural incompatibility between people from different ethnic backgrounds. The science of race read from pigment, cranial feature or hair quality, or culture read from biogeography or gene, has been discredited, unable to support assertions of biological and behavioural difference between so-called races. The discoveries of genomics, increasingly publicized in popular culture, confirm that some 98 per cent of the human genetic pool is shared with chimpanzees, and that variations in DNA sequence are greater within than

---

[3] Winant's argument is not that the forms of racism remain the same. Indeed, he is quick to acknowledge that new ideas and practices of race have arisen in the twenty-first century, including: a postcolonial consciousness tangled up with continued social differentiation on racial lines; the rise of a genomic science that questions racial identity and is mobilized for racial profiling and discrimination; a multicultural ethos that is accompanied by backlashes of an ethno-national nature; and a new Western imperialism that espouses tolerance for the domesticated other and vengeance towards the unassimilated other. See also Bernasconi and Lott (2000), for a helpful synthesis of how thinking in the West has developed since Herder and Kant in the eighteenth century.

between human groups, with residual genetic differences distributed in no consistent or meaningful way to justify racial classification.

Yet it is ironic that the very science that questions race as a marker of human difference is being mobilized to validate physical or behavioural differences between ethnic groups as genetically coded, instead of casting doubt on the validity of such categorization itself.[4] Just as a new 'probabilistic not deterministic, open not closed' biology arises, 'not identifying an essential racial truth that determines individuals to different fates' (Rose, 2007: 161), so too does an interest in linking particular social and medical pathologies to the genetic make-up of individuals located in their supposed ethnic families, thereby endorsing a new politics of race that can claim that South Asians are more prone to heart disease and African-Caribbeans to obesity and social deviance (Duster, 2003; Carter, 2007; Fullwiley, 2007). New genetic advances are simultaneously rebutting and reinforcing the idea of race, breathing new life into biological racism as employers, health insurers, medical authorities and immigration authorities become tempted to select between different ethnic groups on the basis of their alleged weaknesses and vulnerabilities.

To an extent, the return of this particular racial habit can be explained as a failure of categorical displacement: the science of race may have changed, but not the classificatory practices, the durability of coding difference as

---

[4] This is happening, for example, through genetic profiling of given racial and ethnic groups, to see if some of them are more open to heart disease, obesity, crime or educational under-achievement. Through such causal association between medical condition and race/ethnicity, the new science has become an unwitting ally in tracing maladies deep into the genetic core of 'African-Caribbeans', 'Caucasians' or 'Asians'; called to action for race-inflected remedy – curative or punitive – and to comment on the strength and evolutionary prospect of different types of 'racial' stock.

racial. Such obduracy, resurgence, uptake – the social receptivity of racial narration – needs to be explained, and its implications soberly considered. The example of biological racism, that of continuity after the collapse of the racial state in South Africa, of countless cases of racist resurgence at the slightest excuse, prompt reflection on whether there is a temporal logic to race, a dynamic that maintains racial legacies close enough to the surface to spring back with force. What might be the nature of this logic and its workings? Similarly, the examples invite consideration of the forces that regulate the intensities of racial legacy in a given present. The harms of race are never the same in time and space, and, in general, the variability has been considered as the product of the situation, of the swirl of forces in a given conjuncture. But could it be that the intensities are also affected by openings in the present that regulate aspects of the past that get through? If so, an inquiry into the historical freight of race can help to guide anti-racist action in ways that might contain the harms of duration.

This chapter takes up these questions,[5] prompted by the need to make sense of the current racial situation in the West, which has become extraordinarily punitive towards the racialized stranger, and especially Muslims, in the wake of 9/11. It seeks to understand why the steady gains of multiculturalism and the politics of diversity in general, which brokered a kind of truce between majorities and minorities in the last decades of the twentieth century, melted away so fast. It tries to take stock of and locate the enduring habits of racial coding that flow into the encounter between strangers and drag back the open curiosities and possibilities of the encounter into familiar hierarchies

---

[5] These are large and difficult questions to which only partial and sometimes incomplete answers are provided, but in the spirit of soliciting a much-needed debate on the play between past and present in the regulation of race.

of racialized judgement. It reintroduces fragments from the archaeology of race (Tolia – Kelly, 2010) that charge bodily relations in the here and now (adding weight to work on the body as a crucial site of cultural politics). In so doing, however, the chapter also proposes – against the normative turn towards the bodily and the interpersonal – that there are limits to an anti-racist politics based on altering affective relations between strangers.

The chapter opens with a genealogical argument, suggesting that in matters of race, coding habits from the past are deeply etched into the institutional and social unconscious, rushing to the fore during times of disruption to particular settlements of race (authoritarian, liberal, assimilationist, multicultural). The second part of the chapter, however, goes on to argue that the harms of what gets through are regulated by the biopolitics of a given moment, by the specifics of state management of populations (that define insiders and outsiders and their respective treatment). The claim, therefore, is that it is the interplay between phenotypical racism (Saldanha, 2007) – exemplified by a historical vernacular of reading social worth from bodily differences – and racial biopolitics, that critically affects the real experience of race, arbitrating between stranger tolerance and aversion (Wilson, 2009). The collapse of multiculturalism and the rapid spread of xenophobic sentiment today are explained as the result of reinforcing feedbacks between everyday habits of judgement, guided by ingrained legacies of white superiority and an unashamedly punitive state politics of surveillance and discipline of the stranger that has emerged since 9/11. The final part of the chapter discusses the implications of this interpretation for anti-racist practice. Noting the obduracy of negative race sentiments and the force of contemporary biopolitical developments, doubts are raised about the efficacy of a politics of recognition and reconciliation, in favour of a politics that allows the stranger autonomy but also strives for a unity of common cause and solidarity in the face of radical uncertainty.

Archaeology of the Present

In her book *The Nick of Time*, Elizabeth Grosz (2004) opens an important window on the temporal logic of race, by turning to three of the most significant late nineteenth- and early twentieth-century theorists of the evolutionary process. From Darwin, she extracts the principle of time as the generator of newness and unpredictable change, based on his observation that natural and sexual selection lean towards categorical disruption (even among humans) and increased variety, owing to past causal connections combining in novel ways. Accordingly, the evolutionary process – cultural or biological – should not be seen as the realization of an innate logic of nature or vanquishing selection dynamic, but as a generator of variation for no reason, excess rather than fitness and continual change rather than fixity. Grosz's reading of Darwin makes for an understanding of racial evolution as anything other than fixed, predestined or geared towards the preservation of particular classes of human.

Grosz also turns to Nietzsche, who criticized Darwin for seeing too much novelty and variety in the free play of nature, thereby ignoring the 'untimely' force or 'will to power' within every form of life to conserve or expand itself. Otherwise the burden of preservation would prove too onerous, always requiring wasteful new energy to ensure survival. Although Nietzsche imagined this force to be inherent to life, he did not see its release as automatic, but dependent upon supreme human or transcendental effort to commit the future to repetition. Nietzsche's idea of the 'Overman' or force of eternal return, which he did not link to the imperative to preserve/expand nation or race, has been grossly misappropriated in the modern history of race to justify the suppression or elimination of so-called weaker or impure races. Grosz keeps Nietzsche at a safe distance from the barbarisms of racial engineering in the twentieth century, but for the discussion here on the historicity of race the idea of repetition is worth preserving.

Finally, in the opening between temporality, conceived as proliferation or as eternal return, Grosz turns to Bergson's conceptualization of the past as immanence, a duration of the more than necessary into the present as a vital force that only becomes manifest when actualized. Bergson described this force as the *élan vital*, which he did not see as a generic life force but as an 'initial impetus', something of the past acting to delay, prolong and redirect the energies of the present; a spark for 'novelty, invention into what is otherwise predictable' (Grosz, 2004: 201). From a Bergsonian perspective, if race works as duration, it does so as a latent force – bursting through 'a nick in time' that disrupts a settled pattern of life – but in always emergent and unexpected ways because actualization is never the manifestation of a pre-formed latent condition, but the product of past and present combining in novel ways.

This reading of evolution as newness, repetition or immanence suggests three temporalities of race. One is race as a continual unsettlement of categorical divisions and combinations, owing to the restlessness of an evolutionary process heading towards proliferation and variety. The second is the repetition of sameness if the will to power is strong, reigning in newness and variety through some form of machinic organization. The third alludes to the potentiality of the past; accumulations of race that are latent, always a call on the present and ready to be instantiated in unknown ways. There is a danger in shoehorning the genealogy of race into ultimately general abstractions of Time, especially given the contested status of race, but awareness of the different ways in which the past potentiates the present can help to explain the constancies and surprises of race, the temporal freight of racial legacy. To be alerted to the remainders of race in this way is to be drawn to the possibility that a given race 'event' contains more than what is disclosed, poised between gathered momentum and disruption, between the singularity of the will to power and the pluralism of the *élan vital*, between immanence and actualization.

How does this temporal balance work in the history of race? Could it be argued that with the forces of repetition as strong and purposeful as they have been in the modern history of the West[6] – a history in which racial categorization and evaluation has been both pervasive and deeply etched into institutional and popular practice – the propensities of proliferation or recombination identified by Darwin and Bergson are somehow stifled by an actively sustained call to order? Might such an account help to explain why every act of categorical subversion or anti-racist progress is so often folded back into stacked legacies of racism, if not in form then in intent, keeping more or less the same bodies in place? At the end of her book, Grosz turns to Darwin, Nietzsche and Bergson to outline a positive politics of race (and gender), respectful of the past, recognizing latencies yet to be actualized, finding hope in the unpredictability of the evolutionary process. She finds, in their theorizations of time, lessons about the past that could strengthen anti-racist practice.

I share Grosz's normative interest in the historical process, which is all too readily forgotten in the heat of struggle in a given time and place, but would query any imputed equivalence between the temporalities identified. I am suggesting that, in the history of race, the relationship between various evolutionary tendencies may be a hierarchical one, with entrenched genealogies of race acting as

---

[6] My emphasis here on Western racism is not intended as a denial of the social organization by race or ethnicity in non-Western societies, but is a function of the focus of the paper on the West, in particular Europe. There are far too many examples of such organization in the course of African, Latin American and Asian history to sustain a denial of this sort, although the extensive and deep 'naturalization' of white order, through institutional and vernacular practices honed in long and far-reaching histories of Western cultural, political and economic imperialism, is a distinction that lies at the heart of the historical pessimism of this chapter.

a break on emergent novelties and hidden latencies. To propose this is not to read the future of race as more of the same, or to throw a veil of doom around anti-racist politics – inaction in the face of new inventions to maintain and make mischief out of racial hierarchy (as described in the next section). Instead, it is to recognize the weight of embedded racial legacies, to ask why, in our times, progressive openings such as hope for a non-racial society in South Africa after apartheid remain so fragile and vulnerable, why the steady steps towards a multicultural West prior to 9/11 have come to be so quickly swept aside by new racisms building on old exclusions.

If a historical momentum behind an event pushes for more rather than less race, how this works needs to be explained. There is a rich tradition of academic, documentary and fictional writing that alludes to racist continuity, if not in form then certainly in substance, but it tends to fall short of providing an adequate explanation. I do not pretend otherwise here, but wish to suggest that the repetitions of racial hierarchy are assured by the interplay of institutional continuities and ingrained race-coded classificatory practices among humans. Codification and institutionalization are the staples of racial legacy, stretching their tentacles across time through visual and literary cultures, state practices of human categorization, pedagogical traditions, myths of nation, people, community and belonging, technologies of social ordering, and long sedimentations of public culture. These are the staples that kick in well before free will to demarcate, position and embody difference and the stranger. They form the machinery of human selection and ordering whose dead weight repeats the racial society (Rutherford, 2007).

In *Society Must Be Defended*, Michel Foucault (2003) touched on the continuities, complicities and paradoxes of racial ordering by suggesting that the development of decentred – and often subjugated – knowledges in Europe after the late Middle Ages, in reaction to the Roman idea of history as sovereign continuity, introduced a new idea of history as a war between 'races'. Foucault argues that this idea, mobilized by those seeking freedom from oppression as well as those looking to rule in new ways, gradually became normalized as the basis of human and social differentiation through various forms of state and popular classificatory conventions (see also Mendieta, forthcoming). Foucault's thesis on the historical 'ontologization' of race as a given of social differentiation helps to explain the continuities of race beyond forced impositions such as apartheid, through its allusion to institutional and vernacular practices of naturalization (e.g., the colour-coding of understandings of personhood, social worth or citizenship in the narratives, rules and habits of liberal societies).

The naturalization of race occurs through sorting mechanisms, societal and embodied, that trigger the reception of human difference – in the flicker of an eyelid, the hint of a smell, the trace of an utterance – as a sentiment of race. The linkage between precognitive categorization and sensory stimulation envelopes the race-inflected encounter with affective charge, such that in an instance reception becomes an act of categorization, evaluation and emotional response (Ahmed, 2004). If there is a biological instinct among humans to distinguish foe from friend, threat from safety, the familiar from the strange, it could be conjectured that the social machinery of racial classification builds in race as a trigger of this instinct, with race-associated physical attributes as stimuli of territorial demarcation and protection. Accordingly, racial practice becomes an everyday 'doing', effortlessly weaving together historically honed folk summaries that people carry in their head concerning others, along with a phenomenology of bodily response that also recurs with uncanny categorical consistency (Brubaker, Loveman and Stamatov, 2004).

Following Saldanha (2006), this everyday doing of race can be described as 'phenotypical', reliant on quick-fire sensory/affective evaluation of bodily performances as racially meaningful. Two examples of recent work illustrate this kind of sorting mechanism. One is Arun Saldanha's (2007) *Psychedelic Whiteness*, a book on the performance of white superiority on the beaches of Goa through projections of personal biography, colour, posture, dress code, bodily marking, accent, consumption habits and patterns of occupancy of the beach. Saldanha shows how bodily codes, effortlessly locating race and social worth through phenomenological stimulation, tacitly sort out seasoned whites from Britain and Northern Europe, or aspirants from Southern Europe, from Goans and other Asians who, despite their every effort to appear and act 'cool', remain uneasy, second-best, beachcombers. It is through the body rituals that tap into long histories of racial positioning – embodied, discursive, symbolic, and institutional – that the beach becomes a white space, decentring the achievements of postcolonial Goa, making the beach habits of natives and white pretenders seem out of place.

The second illustration is provided by ethnographic work on the embodied performance of race in the former mill towns of northern England that are marked by racial divisions (Alexander, 2004; Swanton, 2007). For the briefest of moments during the protests in 2001 by young South Asian men in towns such as Burnley, Bradford and Oldham – when officials and the media found themselves off-guard, unclear whether these were civic, youth or race riots, and were keen to understand motive – commentary focused on the role of local legacies of racism, ethic segregation and deprivation, cultural and religious isolationism, and paternalist leadership within the Asian community. Behind any interest in the daily lives of whites and Asians lay a desire to grasp the underlying causes of the disturbances, in the hope of formulating policies to address the problems of disadvantage, disaffection, racism and cultural isolation. For a while the judgements of phenotypical racism – local and in the wider public sphere – were suspended or overshadowed by a desire to get behind the facts. This did not last long. As the towns settled back into daily life, and as the scrutiny of Muslims intensified after 9/11 and 7/7 in the so-called war on terror, the stereotypes of phenotype – new heaped upon old – kicked back in vernacular and official discourse, casting the Asians along with Muslims elsewhere in Britain, as cultural aliens and threats to the nation. The racialization of aversion, stepped up to new levels of anxiety, suspicion, fear and hate, has relied centrally, as Alexander and Swanton show, on sensing terrorism, radical Islam, sexual slavery, drug trafficking and cultural backwardness from bodily conduct; from fitting bodies into a vicariously fashioned iconography, that of prayer caps, beards, baggy trousers, rucksacks, Yorkshire accents, loud music, shiny cars and shabby dwellings, triggering powerful negative feelings.

What is clear from these examples is that phenotypical racism draws on the play between sensory response and precognitive categorization, leading to judgements of people whose differences are considered essential to their identity (Hacking, 2005: 111). Its durability lies in the constancy of sensing human difference as racial hierarchy, in the mapping of historical practices of racialization on the human compulsion to categorize. This constancy cannot be traced to genetic make-up and inheritance,[7] since what needs to be explained is not a biological phenomenon but, rather, a race-inflected categorizing culture and its reproduction. The beginnings of an answer may be found in the power of bioscopic regimes, linking normality and abnormality, beauty and ugliness, civilization and barbarism, strength and weakness, health and disease, to particular bodies and bodily states. The details of physiology and behaviour repeatedly picked out by bioscopic regimes

---

[7] Contemporary developments in genomic science show clearly that possibilities and probabilities are transmitted between generations, and always through inflections of culture and praxis, so even those traits with relatively firm genetic associations – and to list racial prejudice among these traits would require considerable proof – come with few guarantees of outcome (Rose, 2007).

as approximations of essential identity and associated standing become etched into the thoughts, actions and feelings of the condemning and the condemned, as Fanon (1967) so acutely observed, through the stories told, the imaginaries circulated, the rules naturalized, and the practices repeated over and again.

In the repetitions of perception, categorization and affect strung together in definitive ways, bioscopic regimes make and sustain 'racial instincts': differences assumed to be 'natural', sentiments triggered by 'racial' information and physiology read as culture. They make racial sensing a tool of everyday orientation, and they ensure its transmission across the generations. Thinking along these lines invites reflection on why particular senses come to the fore in different historical periods, allowing, for example, Western racism to emerge from an ocular sensibility that modernity privileged as a standard of beauty and humanity, as Cornel West (2003) has suggested. Once in place, a bioscopic regime can invent new modalities of race such as the association between blackness and servitude, which arose during the seventeenth century but now lingers long after the abolition of slavery, as the practice of indexing human worth to visual traits becomes standardized (Martino, 2002; Alcoff, 2006).

Duration and Biopolitics

This is a far from complete or proven explanation of the repetitions of race, but its intention is to underline the persistence of honed vernaculars of racial judgement. However, it is also the case, as the two preceding examples imply, that the harms of phenotypical racism vary in intensity in space and time. The Goan example resounds with the echoes of white superiority, gathered around the many manners of self-elevation cultivated during and since colonialism, oscillating between benign curiosity and condescension towards locals who are now recast as strangers in their own land through the encounter. The English example is freighted with menace, its racial coding intent on condemning, crushing the body that offends. It is anything but tacit, imprecise or tolerant. These differences are important, for they not only shape human experience in a given context, but they also suggest the presence of other mediators of race; mediators that regulate the difference between a phenotypical racism looking down upon the marked body and one looking to discipline it.

I wish to suggest that the balance is regulated by biopolitics, by (state) regimes of governing populations (Rai, 2004). Clearly, past debris, everyday negotiations, orders of discipline and strategies of resistance and opposition are all entangled together in the experience of race. But the moderation of past 'excess' – latency becoming manifest, novelty bursting through, history repeating itself, race taking on new meanings and charges – seems to be strongly conditioned by the weight placed on race by given regimes of human governance. Phenotypical racism became deadly when it was harnessed to state mobilizations of biological racism under apartheid, other forms of ethno-nationalism, and colonial rule. Similarly, cultural racism, involving declarations by states and societies that ethnic groups are culturally incompatible, shifts the vernacular of racism decidedly towards strategies of avoidance, ejection and separation of the marked body. The tools of biopolitics, which include racial science, visual economy, standards of classification, habits of public commentary, regimes of discipline, and laws on race and migration, define the norms of personhood, citizenship and integration, the demarcations of home, nation and the outside, the contours of who counts for what. Biopolitical regimes, it can be argued, regulate the state of alert towards the stranger through their specific rules – declared and tacit – of population management. These rules condition which aspects of the racial debris from the past pass through in a nick in time, and, in turn, whether collective feelings towards the stranger veer towards wariness or vilification.

Our times of heightened anxiety towards minorities and outsiders provide a good illustration of the regulatory force of biopolitics. In the West, for example, into old rituals of condemnation of non-whites, Jews and gypsies are being incorporated asylum seekers, migrants, Muslims, militant youths, pan-handlers, carriers of transmissible diseases; no longer seen by majorities as victims of hazard and risk, but as unwanted and threatening strangers, the new black (Kundnani, 2007; Hughes, 2007). This shift is closely linked to the sharp escalation of racial biopolitics after 9/11 as the staple of a politics of community and community security. Bodily traits and 'ethnic' cultures are becoming the basis upon which peoples are allocated rights, identities and a place in the world (Mamdani, 2004; Bayart, 2005), at the expense of other modes of marking community and negotiating difference (e.g., doctrinaire principles, ideas of good citizenship, moral and ethical values). Emblematic of this development is the warning from intellectuals, publics and states of a calamitous war to come between the world of secular liberalism (conveniently traced to the skins and traditions of Europe and North America) and the world of religious society (conveniently traced to the skins and traditions of Islam and rarely those of Christian fundamentalism).

It takes such reasoning to explain how quickly, on the back of the terrorist campaigns of the few, the lives of so many Muslims in the West have come under scrutiny and been ultimately condemned, in the name of safeguarding a population and a 'historic' way of life. This reduction of the choice between the profane and the sacred, the safe and the hazardous, to the traits and practices of particular humans rendered strange, is the work of a biopolitics fanning a vernacular racism that digs deep into old white anxieties of the Orient, Muslims in particular. Past and new portrayals of threat and contamination are being given bite by states, as they hastily cobble together emergency powers permitting intrusive surveillance, arrest without warrant, illegal detention and foreign rendition,

supported by hysterical phenotypical commentary calling
for vigilance of veils, rucksacks, Urdu, gatherings in
mosques, Islamic organizations, and the behaviour of
Muslim-looking people in public and private.[8]

Through these shifts, a late twentieth-century multicultural politics of recognition and co-habitation has been
swept aside by a politics of aversion in which states and
publics feel morally unperturbed in demanding an end to
veils, religious schools, and the linguistic and cultural isolation of minorities. Linked to an alarmist discourse of
collective preservation and national security, it is hardly
surprising that the new disciplinary developments are
accompanied by the kind of phenotypical racism emerging
in places like Burnley, Oldham and Bradford. Under such
a biopolitics, the taming of the errant body – in this case
the Muslim body – is urged as a necessity, a matter of
everyday vigilance from the responsible citizen, shamed for
thinking and doing otherwise. The biopolitics of multiculturalism may have essentialized the identities of ethnic
minorities, it may have been smug in assuming the authority to grant rights to the 'deserving' stranger, and it may

---

[8] The message to Muslims in the West is that they can stay 'once they
have divested themselves of what many of them regard as . . . essential
to themselves' (Asad, 2003: 168). This concession too, however, is
qualified. 'Bad Muslims' can only become 'good Muslims' (Mamdani,
2004), and never fully of the West, as those doing the judging come to
redefine the world – once again – as the battleground between a peaceful, progressive, rational and tolerant West and its opposite in the
Islamic East (Gregory, 2004). Between the one and the other stereotype
– both called to justify disciplinary action – there is no possibility of
Muslims being subjects with varying, complex and multiple identities,
living in the West to integrate, improve their lot, claim the public turf
like other citizens, be allowed to belong to communities of their choice,
mixing the reverent and secular, traditional and modern in a quest for
a richer and fuller life (Modood, 2005; Nederveen Pieterse, 2007). That
being Muslim in the West might amount to being quite ordinary, on
the right side of civilization, has become a matter of proving it, and
against the odds.

have done more to recognize the cultural autonomy of minorities than to meet their material needs (Brown, 2006; Fortier, 2008; Hage, 1998; Ahmed, 2007), but it did not condone a culture of vigilantism and punishment.

The new biopolitics, which specializes in naming and tracking the errant body, provides an opening for past racisms to return, wherever a politics of the social/communal is being redefined as a politics of disciplining minorities and strangers. Whether this biopolitical turn signals a general trend, linked to the end of universal projects that cut across differences of class, gender and ethnicity, is a possibility that cannot be ignored, according to some commentators. For example, Arjun Appadurai (2006: 7) argues that the killings in Rwanda, Bosnia and Gujarat, along with the rage on all sides sparked by the current 'war on terror', are evidence of such a turn. He argues that the cultural mixing and spatial rupture brought about by globalization is producing an 'anxiety of incompleteness' among majorities in different parts of the world; a 'narcissism of minor differences' and a 'fear of small numbers' heightening awareness of difference, as well as violent response towards it. For Appadurai, in this context, minorities have become 'metaphors and reminders of the betrayal of the classical national project' (p. 43), easily tracked through various modes of 'counting, classifying, and surveying populations' (p. 47), such that when 'specific situations become overcharged with anxiety . . . that body [can] be annihilated' (ibid.).

Slavoj Žižek (2008), in contrast, offers a different general explanation for the return of racial biopolitics. For Žižek, an ideology-based politics, which coalesced around differences of value and aspiration, has been displaced by a politics of 'efficient administration of life' that sees the disciplining of 'deviant' modes of conduct (from civic disloyalty to sexual freedom and deviancy) traced to particular bodies (from asylum seekers to immigrants and minorities) as the staple of community maintenance. Žižek explains:

Today's predominant mode of politics is *post-political bio-politics* – an awesome example of theoretical jargon which, however, can easily be unpacked: 'post-political' is a politics which claims to leave behind old ideological struggles and, instead, focus on expert management and administration, while 'bio-politics' designates the regulation of the security and welfare of human lives as its primary goal. It is clear how these two dimensions overlap: once one renounces big ideological causes, what remains is only the efficient administration of life . . . *almost* only that. That is to say, with the depoliticised, socially objective, expert administration and coordination of interests as the zero level of politics, the only way to induce passion into this field, to actively mobilise people, is through fear, a basic constituent of today's subjectivity. For this reason, bio-politics is ultimately a politics of fear, it focuses on defence from potential victimisation or harassment. (p. 34; emphasis in original)

Such a politics of fear, according to Žižek (see also Bauman, 2007), relies on maintaining a public culture of anxiety over questions of national identity and security, the rights and obligations of immigrants, the moral and cultural bearings of the nation, and the collective traditions to be defended. It has to name the deviant body and prepare either for its domestication through various practices of integration, or for its exclusion through tight surveillance and discipline. It returns bodily difference, and above all the selections and feelings of race, to the centre of politics.

The reformulation of the politics of community as a politics of the deviant body is being reinforced by another general shift in state practice. This is the displacement of an approach that sought to avoid or insure against future hazard and risk, by a regime of catastrophe management that judges the perils to be both potentially devastating and unavoidable (see chapter 6). Propped up by anxious warnings from governments, experts and the media, this political turn hinges on a discourse of the threat of total destruction – by mutant germs or genes, super-intelligent machines, climate change, global terrorism, speculative capitalism gone mad, or masses on the move. Instead of avoidance and insurance, it recommends mitigation and preparedness, under the leadership of a 'security state' that can build resilience and facilitate recovery (Lakoff, 2007; Dillon, 2008). Increasingly costly interventions, including tidal barriers, banking bailouts, high-tech surveillance, mass vaccinations and disaster simulation exercises are justified as an exercise in catastrophe management rather than prevention, probabilistic rather than certain.

There is little ambiguity, however, over the place of the deviant body in the politics of catastrophe management. The state of permanent alert requires the enemy to be named and personified, so that majorities can be assured that the threatening body is known, tracked and eliminated. Proclaiming the urgencies of mitigation and preparedness, governments are suspending, without debate or justification, the hard-fought protocols of proof, legality, and civil or human right that formerly guided state action towards citizens and non-citizens in the liberal democracies. It has become easy to round up, imprison or eliminate imprecisely defined suspects on grounds of national security, community cohesion, risk mitigation and efficient management of life. The balance between two historic modes of disaster management that Adi Ophir (2007) writes about – the 'providential state' striving for the welfare of all, including migrants and minorities, and the 'catastrophic state', ready to 'wipe out, when it deems necessary, any particular individual, or a multitude of anonymous ones' (p. 21) – is tilting decidedly towards the second form. 'The administration of disaster' as 'a form of governance and a way of ruling,' involving the suspension of 'citizenship, the system of law and the constitution itself' (ibid.), is being taken for granted as states of emergency cease to be seen as states of exception.

Whatever the causes of the contemporary scaling-up of punitive biopolitics (from anxieties of globalization to the politics of life or catastrophe management), the new tactics of order, playing on popular fear and aversion towards people considered different or anomalous, are allowing all manner of vengeance to be thrown at the racialized stranger (Terranova, 2007) – though not all strangers, by any means. The cosmopolitan, if urbane, culturally dextrous, articulate, light-footed, and well connected, is largely left alone to contribute to the multicultural nation as doctor, nurse, engineer, teacher, waiter or knowledge worker. He or she tends to be pursued only by the nationalist perennially worrying about the decline of the ethnic nation, or by the security state when suspected of seditious intent. Instead, it is the most visible, vulnerable, needy, ill-equipped stranger who is most at risk. For this stranger – graded by colour and cultural affinity to the mythic community – the combination of intrusive state surveillance and raw phenotypical racism can only mean universal condemnation.

Negotiating Race

Although this chapter has placed its emphasis on the historical continuities of race, it has also argued that the actual experience of race is strongly shaped by the biopolitical present. The difference between feeling awkward on a beach for not appearing hip and being removed for it is important, as is the difference between neighbours from different ethnic backgrounds gossiping about each other and attacking each other, or that between states demanding conformity from visible minorities and rounding them up. These are differences of life and death, possibility and impossibility, inclusion and ejection, and they have a direct bearing on the aims, ambitions and prospects of anti-racist struggle in a given time and place. The ontological pessimism of this chapter, grounded in the consistency of race as a mode of human sorting, therefore, is not an argument against anti-racism. It is, if anything, reason to think carefully about what is possible under conditions of racial persistence and in nicks in time regulated by particular biopolitical intensities, which is what this last section attempts.

To begin with, the potency of race as a living legacy forces sharp questions about a future liberated from racial categorization (e.g., a 'planetary humanism' as proposed by Paul Gilroy, 2001). If phenotypical racism is as ingrained as I have suggested it to be, the quest for a non-racial future may prove to be elusive or long in coming, for it would have to draw on a counter-legacy of human judgement that renders race anomalous in institutional and vernacular practice. To suggest this is not to stop criticizing racial thought and practice, exposing the harms and injustices – past and present – of racial legacy, learning from the past or looking to it for alternative evolutionary tendencies (as Grosz suggests), or building other modes of human recognition in order to delimit racial categorization. Instead, it is to see these efforts as part of a politics of neutralizing rather than transcending race, to not wait for humanity to rise above itself in order to tackle racism. It is to be guided by a pragmatic interest in flattening and decentring racial hierarchies, for example, by preventing phenotypical racism from becoming harmful or by disarming the machinery of racial biopolitics, as outlined below.

Regarding the performances of phenotype, everyday mixity of itself, as shown by the Goan and English examples, does not guarantee the conversion of a vernacular of racial aversion into one of tolerance or recognition. However, an understanding of the space of encounter – physical or virtual – as one in which strangers meet as equals can force the suspension of condemnation, perhaps even encourage majority acceptance of the right of minorities and strangers to claim the shared space. The harms of phenotypical racism intensify when public legitimacy is given to the treatment of certain bodies as inferior, a threat and out of place; harbouring feelings of superiority and righteousness on one side of the divide, and feelings of inferiority, indebtedness or resentment on the other side.

Interventions that normalize a public culture of equal subjectivity can help to dismantle the hierarchical assumptions
that regulate the quality of response to difference.

Organizing for equal subjectivity in the field of race is
a matter of acting across a range of fairly familiar institutional, interpersonal and symbolic arenas. This includes
building consensus behind stringent anti-racist laws, progressive immigration and integration policies, and race-
sensitive regulations in such fields as education, employment,
welfare and public culture. It includes, as suggested in the
preceding chapter, local interventions to build a sense of
the commons and studied trust among strangers without
assuming any magic of interpersonal empathy. It includes
developing a counter-culture that visualizes the racial past
and present in novel ways, exposing its harms as a clear
violation (in the way that photography did during the US
civil rights struggles of the 1960s), showing the absurdity
of reducing the other to flimsy 'essences' of race, publiciz-
ing the long history of interracial connections and commonalities, and promoting hope and compassion as public
sentiments (Hariman, 2009b). Such interventions can be
seen as tactics of containment, working to restrict the
violence of phenotypical racism, strengthen the disempow-
ered, cultivate other modes of phenotypical judgement,
build cultures of co-habitation, and change the sentiments
of communal existence. They can be seen as fragile, temporary and renewed acts of the present, holding back the
rushes of racial legacy.

To turn to the biopolitical, the current state of emergency in the West demands a radical change to state practices of national integration if the stranger is to be seen as
anything other than disruptive, a threat. The vexed question is whether this should involve more than a return to
the politics of recognition that had come to the fore prior
to 9/11, which, in its multicultural guise, looked to
acknowledge difference, promote inclusion and encourage
new sympathies. Its reply to racist biopolitics, curiously,
was an alternative kind of body politics (though never

described as such), one that focused on the particularity of the stranger and on the ethic of living together (Naidoo, 2008; Dalal, 2008; Ahluwalia, 2007).[9] It replaced a mid-twentieth-century anti-racism that focused on tackling the structural and institutional sources of racism, for example, by strengthening anti-racist legislation, combating racial abuse and discrimination, and ensuring minority access to work, welfare and rights. It also saw the challenge of race as part of a broader problem, namely, the systemic reproduction of class, gender and other forms of inequality in capitalist society. By the late twentieth century, such a struggle for sameness, pursued largely through the impersonal, gave way to one attentive to difference and particularity, criticized for its inattentiveness to the specificities of race, culture and the personal.

In closing this chapter, I ask if a new humanism alone can tackle the violent incursions of the emergency state. Bhikhu Parekh (2008) writes that living in a divided but interdependent world requires the cultivation of an ethos of common humanity, through the vigorous pursuit of certain core principles. These include sanctioning self-interest when it harms others (regardless of territorial and cultural location), acting 'together in the spirit of human solidarity' (p. 226), and accepting engagement as the 'very condition of one's growth' (p. 227). His suggestions echo those of many writers who turn to the essentials of living among others to extract the core political principles of the open society, for example, the idea that human subjectivity arises out of being with others (Kristeva, 1993; Nancy, 2000; Levinas, 1998) and therefore demands in its own

---

[9] One reason for a turn to a politics of ethics – the desire to link moral and political philosophy – is the belief that rationalism, utilitarianism, consumerism and individualism have diminished the role of ethics in social organization and human interaction, and that credos such as liberalism, socialism, religious society and nationalism have legitimated harm, including ethical harm, towards those believed to be on the outside (Appiah, 2006; Parekh, 2000).

right a responsibility towards the stranger (Amin, 2004), or the idea that the specialized or divided society requires compelling emblems of solidarity such as sympathy, hospitality or fraternity in order to flourish (Smith, 1759, Derrida, 2002; Ricoeur, 1994; Rutherford, 2007). 'Ethical humanism' does not take subjectivity, citizenship or community as given, tied to the primacies of race, ethnicity, tradition or nation. Instead, it ties membership to ethical practice towards the other, a right to be earned by all who find themselves placed together in a society, and not applying only to its strangers and minorities, a theme developed further in the next chapter.

In the current climate of unashamed vengefulness towards certain humans, it would be ill judged and untimely to criticize a politics of belonging that emphasizes the rights of personhood, human fellowship and an ethic of care.[10] The question, however, is whether ethical humanism possesses the strength and persuasiveness to tackle the machinic force of emergency biopolitics, daily embedding a culture of aversion towards the stranger through everyday surveillance and discipline, software-based sorting and bureaucratic selection, state restrictions on movement and entitlements, unquestioned corporate discriminations, and unrestrained public commentary (Graham, 2010). A politics of human fellowship may be able to put a face to

---

[10] The affective potential of such a politics should not be underestimated, especially when we consider how centrally biopolitics relies on the engineering of passions. Anne-Marie Fortier (2008) shows this in her account of how multicultural and assimilationist policies in Britain have tapped into a structure of national feelings of fear, anxiety, love and hope through which minorities and majorities sense each other and their place in the nation. The policies, in actively defining citizenship, community and national values, animate popular response to difference and divergence. A politics of personhood filtered through state management of feelings has anything but a background regulatory influence. It determines whether the stranger is felt as friend or foe, outsider or insider, anomalous or ordinary.

the malpractices of this machinery, expose its hidden ethic of human treatment and lay down the guidelines for an alternative system of social integration, but it lacks the means to stop or subvert the disciplinary routines.

It is also worth remembering that the biopolitics of emergency possesses its own moral force, pleading for ethical responsibility towards legacy, the community to be protected and the future to be defended, through collective action against those deemed to pose a threat. It too uses the language of solidarity and community to select between the good and the bad, building powerful moral and affective impetus behind the choice to discipline particular human subjects in the name of liberty, justice and security. This is how the violence and injustice of the emergency state towards the racialized other is reworked, apprehended by majorities as an ethics of peace, survival and responsibility towards both 'us' and 'them' (Brown, 2006; Žižek, 2008). In these circumstances, wielding ethical humanism as a weapon against the passionately felt sentiments of emergency 'management' – appealing to human fellowship when biopower cloaks its own might in the same language – could amount to tickling an adversary in armour-plate with a feather.

Thinking beyond the humanist turn in anti-racist politics is patchy and underdeveloped, but desperately needed to contain the contemporary escalations of race. A first step would be to expose the hidden architecture of racial discipline that drives the politics of emergency, to build moral outrage and political momentum against its injuries and exclusions, to campaign to bring state disciplinary practices under legal and democratic control, to impose a thousand checks on inflammatory labelling, excessive surveillance and draconian punishment, and to reaffirm the benefits of a 'providential' model of security, well-being and social integration (to borrow Ophir's phrase). A new politics of 'managing' diversity and mobility in an age of risk and uncertainty needs to be developed, one that rejects crude racializations of threat, stops profiteering from the exaggeration of hazard and dispenses with a model of security based on the vilification of the stranger.

Accordingly, at one end of a new anti-racist movement, sustained effort is required to expose the damage, danger and absurdity of a machinery of governance – visible and invisible – so reliant on coding, tracking and disciplining the vicariously defined errant body. This requires the anti-racist struggle to expand its coverage so that the harms of different forms of racial labelling (biological, cultural, phenotypical) are clearly grasped, as are the needs of the diverse groups of people who become 'racialized' (from ethnic and religious minorities to asylum seekers and migrants). It also requires the anti-racist movement to see itself as part of a broader coalition of interests opposed to other forms of discrimination and aversion, to the erosion of civil and political liberties, and to the incursions of the security state, working with other forces to break the chain of connections linking census practices, labelling conventions, allocation decisions, surveillance practices, work, immigration and welfare rules, and public discourse. By this chain are trapped the poor, the marginalized, the itinerant, the ill-fitting, the less able, the outsider of different colour and hue, beckoning a politics of common suffering and common cause.

At the other end, the anti-racist movement has to play its part in rethinking the politics of unity and security in a world of heightened diversity, risk and uncertainty. As argued in the last chapter, this requires showing that preparedness is possible without demonizing particular sections of the population or humanity elsewhere and without compromising the principle of universal welfare. This is a preparedness of forensically isolating – and without clamour – those who really pose a threat, displacing the rhetoric of catastrophe by one of managing uncertainty through collective effort, defusing fear, disaffection and envy through dialogue and understanding, and showing that an ethic of inclusion does not compromise state security. Such an expanded anti-racism breaks free from the constraint of tackling aversion only through a politics of human recognition.

Echoing the doubts raised here about the humanist turn, Žižek (2008) goes so far as to propose a politics of distance that is respectful of human difference, disagreement and dissent. A politics of distance runs the risk of inflaming the current situation which thrives on the vilification of the 'abnormal' body, by allowing the harmful phenotypical aversions that have come to the fore to close down the many affects and relationships that humans are capable of (Lim, 2010), in the name of 'respectful' distance. Distance in these circumstances becomes an excuse for disrespect, requiring other forms of intervention in order to ensure that the autonomy of the other is respected. Perhaps the conjugations of a politics of the commons articulated in this book – gathered around the urban unconscious, shared concerns, common affects and aspirations, plural publics, transversal coalitions – can help to ensure that difference and diversity are not seen as a simple choice between hating or loving the stranger.

Interventions in the machinery of biopolitics, harnessed to a politics of the commons, can help to expose and neutralize the harms of racial legacy. This I take to be a central message of the exhibition in Barcelona on apartheid. No one knew when this perverse model of human organization would break down, but gradually its opponents came to know and dismantle its elaborate architecture through many subversive inventions, and steadily they pieced together a vision of the just society that brought people together across the fractures of race and particularist interest. The struggle kept the politics of recognition close to the politics of collective well-being. The severance of this connection seems to have diluted progress towards the equal and shared society in South Africa since the end of apartheid, just as it seems to have narrowed the scope and reach of contemporary anti-racist struggle in the West.

– 5 –
Imagined Community[1]

The fear of the barbarian is what risks making us barbarian.

Todorov, 2010: 6

Introduction

In interrogating the politics of interpersonal ties, this book has examined the affective formation in other relational spaces: the judgements threaded into the bodily encounter, the inducements of place, the feelings formed in intimate publics, the affinities of collaborative work, and the proximities with, or enabled by, things and artefacts. The balance of affect towards the stranger – and the world at large – has

---

[1] This chapter expands ideas developed in conjunction with Pep Subirós and others in the Forum of Concerned Citizens of Europe, established in 2010 at the Centre for Contemporary Culture in Barcelona, to raise public awareness of the xenophobic turn in Europe and to develop another manifesto of aspiration and belonging. Details of the ideas – and other activities of the Forum – can be found on the website: ⟨www.livingindiversity.org⟩.

been traced to the viscosity of these spaces and their intensity of habitation, both held to shape meanings of belonging, contours of community, and judgements of similarity and difference. In these relational spaces have been found the habits of living the familiar and the strange. One of the most charged relational spaces is the imagined community, whose materials – from myths and symbols of unity to tools of social integration and public discourses of belonging – profoundly shape personal and collective understanding of the place of strangers. We caught a glimpse of this power in the preceding chapter's account of how national biopolitical regimes regulate the harms of racism.

This chapter considers the contagions of imagined community in more detail, but it does so in the context of an unsettled ideational space, in order to reveal the ambiguous nature of myths of belonging. It focuses on Europe, a public sphere that is sufficiently incomplete to gather new counterforces to repel gathering suspicion and revulsion of the stranger. In focusing on an imagined community whose fixtures are not firm, the aim is not to suggest neutrality but, rather, the value of a politics of active context over the meaning of symbolic togetherness. Europe as an idea of attachment gathers diverse sentiments brewing quietly under the surface, periodically breaking the surface to colonize collective consciousness; today in the form of aversion towards minorities and strangers, exploited by conservative forces with devastating outcomes for the stranger. Yet the fact that such rushes can capture the collective imaginary with affective charge is also reason to hope that alternative sentiments of togetherness might come to the fore in the still imprecise space called Europe. In Europe, unfinished as a collective culture, another sense of unity actively promoted by progressive social movements, political parties, educational and cultural institutions, policy initiatives, and opinion makers, could make a difference – but only if it is able to find affective grip, and secure the same kind of emotional energy that its counterpart has managed to gather.

The chapter readily acknowledges the challenge faced in firing public interest in a non-xenophobic idea of Europe, given a long history of Eurocentric hauteur, the failings of the European public sphere as an intimate public, and the continuing refraction of public sentiment and understandings of risk and security within national cultures and state strategies (Balibar, 2011). However, it also argues that without such a change – underpinned by pragmatic reforms to extend economic and welfare equality, and effort to replenish the European public sphere with felt interest and deliberative energy – there is little chance of resisting the culture of aversion that is spreading across the continent. This culture will not disappear through reason and pragmatic reform, but requires the persuasions of another machinery of feelings, harnessed to another vision of collective living in Europe. Without new sentiments, there will be little momentum behind scripts of minorities and strangers as equals, and, within Europe, no reason for publics to question powerful national and state narratives of belonging that prey on fear and animosity (Todorov, 2010).

To be clear, the interest here does not lie in claiming Europe as a new model of living with diversity for the rest of the world. There has been too much of this kind of projection in the past, to the detriment of the rest of the world, nested in the cruelties of empire and cultural negation. Instead, my aim is to say something about the power of imaginaries and their affective spaces. At the same time, the choice of Europe is not accidental. There is a dark cloud of xenophobia spreading across an irreversibly plural Europe, with worrying internal and external implications. Europe is on the verge of rejecting universalism and multiculturalism as a way of living with diversity, replacing it with a disciplinarian approach towards strangers and minorities.

To draw the bridge in this way will only damage Europe's standing in the world, inflame hostility between majorities and minorities within the continent, weaken Europe's capacity to learn and invent by being in and of the world, and extinguish one important space – material and symbolic – of civilized coexistence and responsibility towards the displaced subject. The stakes are high; reason enough to consider two contrasting imaginaries of living with diversity in Europe – one silently unfolding and the other to be named. Discussion of the alternatives is preceded by a reflection on the nature of the European public sphere so as to outline the ambiguities of Europe as a space of belonging, and followed by a consideration of how the politics of a permissive Europe might proceed.

The European Public Sphere

If a European public sphere exists, its moorings are institutional and procedural rather than popular or affective. The fifty-year history of the European Union has produced a functioning commons but not a felt community. Though the architects of the Union, especially those who saw it as a bulwark against war and totalitarianism, envisioned a Europe of common interests, shared values and interdependencies, yielding an imagined community of tempered national loyalties and strengthened cosmopolitan affiliations, this has not come to pass. The people of Europe – majorities and minorities – do not see themselves as part of a common family or shared public space, and self-labelling as 'European' remains strongly conditional and secondary, as do obligations to others in Europe.

Since the start of EU surveys in 1991, monitoring the strength of people's affiliation to their locality, region, nation and Europe, declarations to the latter have stayed consistently below 30 per cent lower than to the other spaces of affiliation, with never more than 15 per cent expressing a strong attachment to Europe. The strength of attachment to the nation or its local communities remains prevalent, with the advantages and additions of being European barely acknowledged (Pichler, 2008). More fine-grained investigations – for example, a survey of meanings of Europe in four regions in France, Italy, the UK and Finland – uncover a range of opinion: Europe as intrusive, lacking a historical or cultural commons, democratic, plural and tolerant, and enhancing (or not) to individual or collective welfare (Antonsich, 2008). They rarely confirm Europe as an imagined community, a common home or a space of emotional investment. A thin European public sphere exists, without an intimate public. It is one propped up by media and political commentary on EU rules and regulations, firing the public imagination only when national interests are perceived to be at risk. In turn, civic participation tends to be restricted to the activities of non-governmental organizations – social, cultural, environmental, economic, political – in EU policy formation and consultation, and, to a lesser degree, in the delivery of policy decisions. Civil society appears as a cog in the machinery of regulation and governance, and not as an independent force involved in the making of a new transnational order (Kohler-Koch, 2009). Europe lacks a body of active and concerned citizens and interest associations to contribute to the life of the Union through public deliberation, scrutiny of policy decisions and proposals, and proposals that decision-makers and opinion formers cannot ignore – a public sphere of active social identification and involvement.

Europhiles lament the consequences of a rudimentary European public sphere. They consider it to have deprived the EU of a proper demos, able to stir hearts and minds, enact a European commons, ensure political transparency and democratic accountability, articulate common public concerns and interests (e.g., employment, welfare, quality of life, social insurance), and allow the formation of a shared identity based on genuine engagement and collaboration (Delanty and Rumford, 2005; Habermas 2009; Beck and Grande, 2007). They believe that a post-national European public sphere pursued through active civic participation, and supported by appropriate political reforms, will help to displace or supplement national and local cultural attachments and political orientations. This kind of change is considered a precursor of affective public interest in the European project, so that the grip of anti-cosmopolitan sentiment and xenophobic politics can be loosened.

Differences of opinion, thus, tend to focus on whether an active European public sphere requires common values and principles to hold it together. Two claims in particular have proved to be controversial: first, that any unity should court – and constitutionally enshrine – principles of political organization true to Europe, such as those of liberal democracy or the social state (typified by Habermas's proposals on constitutional patriotism); and, second, that deliberation be guided by certain enduring European cultural values (typically, the Europe of reason, caritas, the rule of law, and universal rights). Debate on the European public sphere has settled around these two claims, following a flurry of activity in the early 2000s on the core values of a European Constitution, reactivated shortly thereafter by prominent European intellectuals led by Derrida and Habermas, in protest against the invasion of Iraq in the name of a Europe claimed to stand for peace, solidarity and diplomacy (in contrast to the culture of individualism, fundamentalism and unilateralism driving the conflagration). Strikingly, both the constitutional debate and the Iraq deliberations turned to an old idea: Europe as the land of universal rights and cosmopolitan engagement; care founded in catholic humanism or the welfare state; commitment to the rule of law and to democratic deliberation; and quest for the unknown based on science, inquiry and exploration (Bauman, 2004).

Here, Europe is claimed as a particular kind of demos and civitas, firmly rooted in the history and geography of the continent. The representation of Europe in this essentialist manner has not passed without criticism. The reading of the European demos has been criticized as historically selective and fanciful as a guide for the future; the latter on the grounds that deliberative democracy or constitutional patriotism will fail to motivate publics and political movements in a Europe of strong national traditions holding together peoples who neither see themselves as co-citizens of Europe nor are necessarily loyal to a tradition of deliberation or constitutionalism (Baumeister, 2007). Other commentaries have focused on the limitations of a liberal or deliberative solution for a Europe, judged to require active participatory politics so that shared interests and concerns can arise out of active practices of cross-European citizenship (Beck and Grande, 2007; Outhwaite, 2008).

The criticisms of the nostra of civitas have been more vituperative, for stereotyping both Europe and the rest of the world. The synthesis of Europe as peaceful, humane, reasonable, inquisitive and democratic has provoked accusations of neglecting the continent's own fraught legacy of genocide, militarism, minority oppression and imperialism (Kumar, 2008). It is the absence rather than the presence of the nostra that is understood to explain atrocities such as those in Bosnia and Kosovo, the treatment of less prosperous and new EU member states as second-rate partners, and the failure of the EU to act decisively and in unity during major global geopolitical conflicts (Anderson, 2007). They are also understood to have lain idle – sometimes complicit – in the treatment of immigrants, asylum seekers, minorities and non-conformists as dangerous subjects and tainted citizens (Balibar, 2004; Hansen, 2009). Europe presented as such, by default or intention, is perceived as having allowed political cultures beyond Western Europe (including those of post-socialist Europe – see Shehu, 2011) to be judged as markedly different and somehow inferior.

At the heart of these misgivings lies the concern that an attempt to identify a normative core to Europe risks fixing the idea of Europe in backward-looking ways, along with a denial of affinities with political and public cultures elsewhere. It is this kind of concern that lies behind the liberal critique of a values-based approach, which, instead, settles for a rights-based and procedurally defined public sphere exposed to the settlements of an expanding and overlapping representative democracy. For liberal Europeanists, the challenge for Europe:

> does not mean creating a new positive and singular identity, but rather trying to define a locus of communication and mutual recognition between distinct reflexive national identities. Put differently, 'Europe' is not an end in itself and there are no normative reasons (although there might be pragmatic ones) to privilege some 'European Others' over 'Other Others'. European construction does not herald the end of the states, but it must relativize the absolute dimension of the state by questioning the close association which is made between nationality and citizenship. This would lead to democratizing (not abolishing) borders, i.e., following Etienne Balibar, turning their discriminating function into a function of reciprocity. (Lacroix, 2009: 154)

The liberal argument is as strong as its premise that the integrity of the political process is not compromised. Yet liberal democracy has failed to contain corporatism, rule by elites, obdurate asymmetries of power, motivation and capability, and manipulation by vested and organized interests, which yields coalitions and decisions involving all but the represented subject. These are the granularities of representative democracy that maintain skewed hierarchies of political participation, recognition and reward, ensuring the return of a divided or disinterested public at home, and of minorities within and beyond national boundaries as secondary subjects. Thus, if deliberative rationalism is to be judged too weak to produce a new politics of reciprocity in Europe, liberal democracy must be judged as perhaps too strong in its manipulations, with both leaving unresolved the problem of how a shared political and cultural commons is to be constructed. There may be merit, then, in returning to the idea of Europe by reformulating its normative parameters and expectations, instead of ruling it out on intrinsic or historical grounds.

Might it be worth preserving an idea of Europe that plays on the unity of difference, to avoid the kind of degeneracy that Todorov suggests in the epigraph to this chapter (Todorov, 2010)? The principles of curiosity, care and diplomacy picked out by Derrida, Habermas and Bauman could be claimed less as evidence of the European heritage than as inventions needed to tackle a turbulent and anxious future without resort to aversion and avoidance, with the help of alliances with the stranger. This would amount to an explicit break with the traditional and canonical, a conscious act of disobedience and disruption (Mignolo, 2009). It would express desire for a new and different public sphere and politics of co-presence, a quest to harness the above principles for an 'unimagined' democracy (Balibar, 2004), a new kind of '*global* public sphere, of which European publics are wings' (Young, 2005: 154; emphasis in original). Such a move would defend itself as deliberate organization for a common democratic life, clear that the stranger must be placed on the inside of the arena of agonistic engagement, not wished away. What seems certain is that a thin, procedural European public sphere will not suffice at a time when, through unspoken diffusion, it is being colonized by negative sentiments.

European Xenophobia

Aggressive political demagoguery, targeting minorities, immigrants and democracy itself, is on the march again in Europe. It has spread from fundamentalist and xenophobic outliers to mainstream political forces trying to appease national majorities that have been destabilized by growing economic and welfare insecurity, cultural and ethnic mixity, and future uncertainty. The diffusion across Europe is silent but fast and firm, contributing to the making of a European pubic culture united in its aversion to the discrepant and untraditional. No longer the mischief of the far right in countries such as Britain, France, Italy, Austria, the Netherlands and Hungary, this demagoguery is becoming part of the national consensus in these countries and others, such as Belgium, Denmark, Sweden, Poland, Germany and Switzerland. Europe is adopting a disturbingly uniform tone towards the stranger, heading towards defining itself as a cultural union on negative grounds.

As economic insecurity digs in, along with loss of the guarantees of the social state and intensification of the uncertainties of global exposure and interdependence, so too does xenophobia, normalizing easy labelling and surveillance of the stranger through endless talk in the cultural and political media of greedy asylum seekers, disloyal or seditious immigrants, would-be Muslim terrorists, unassimilated Roma, and a desire to return to the founding principles and values of national or European community (Fekete, 2009). Moved by a persuasive and persistent rhetoric from opinion formers, anguishing about population expansion, stretched resources, community disintegration, and future hazard and risk – phenomena invariably and viscerally traced to particular kinds of subject and subjectivity – majorities, joined by minorities and settled migrants, are learning to reject the outsider and those in need as a matter of course or necessity (Wodak, 2011). A new lexicon of insiders and outsiders, marking out clear spatial and cultural borders of demarcation, has begun to settle as a sorting mechanism that requires no further thought. It blames the victims of unfettered financial speculation, poverty, inequality and authoritarianism at a global scale, and it ignores the fact that the contribution of immigrants and refugees has been, is and will remain essential to European social, economic and cultural life (Azmanova, 2012; Agier, 2011).

The problem has been maturing for some time. In 1997 – the European Year against Racism – the EU commissioned a survey across all 15 member states that uncovered a worrying level of xenophobia and racism, with nearly a third of the majorities contacted openly describing themselves as 'quite racist' or 'very racist' (European Commission, 1997). These attitudes were found to be pronounced in Belgium, Denmark, France and Austria, and less so in Spain, Ireland, Portugal and Sweden, being common in particular to people dissatisfied with their life circumstances, facing the threat of unemployment, insecure about the future, and without confidence in the public and political authorities. Typically, migrants and minorities emerged as the object of fear, anxiety and aversion, forming a threat to the democratic arrangements and the rights and freedoms otherwise valued by respondents. While three-quarters of the respondents declared support for the multicultural society, between a third and half wished the rights of those they considered a 'problem' to be restricted (illegal migrants, those involved in crime, the unemployed and welfare claimants, and minorities with inflexible cultural values). The hapless and unfortunate were beginning to be bunched together with criminals and rogues.

A similar survey six years later (EUMC, 2005) darkened this portrayal, registering a 'significant' increase in support for propositions that multicultural society had reached its limits and that illegal immigrants should be repatriated (shared respectively by 66 per cent and 25 per cent of the respondents). Attitudes towards migrants and minorities had continued to harden, with half the survey expressing its aversion to immigration, a third to asylum, half to diversity and a quarter to ethnic mixing. A significant majority considered ethnic minorities to pose a threat to collective identity and well-being; an intolerance manifest in intense harassment or discrimination of especially the Roma, Muslims and sub-Saharan Africans in public places, in the labour market, and in access to welfare support (European Union Agency for Fundamental Rights, 2009). As before, this pathology of aversion went with an understanding of Europe as liberal. According to another survey, over two thirds of EU citizens believe that they share a set of cultural values that are uniquely European and worth preserving in the face of globalization (European Commission, 2007). The most cited values are peace (61 per cent of respondents), respect for nature and the environment (50 per cent), social equality and solidarity (37 per cent), freedom of expression (37 per cent), and tolerance and openness to others (37 per cent).

Liberal intolerance in Europe works by placing selected strangers in another camp, alien in its practices, worthy of redress in the name of the tolerant society itself (Brown, 2006). Accordingly, negative feelings and associated moves to name and shame, curtail and contain, discipline and eject, domesticate and assimilate, are being defended – indeed deemed necessary – in the name of Europe's liberal heritage. The resulting rough treatment of the stranger is being justified as a necessary measure to preserve an egalitarian, open and tolerant European way of life (Lentin, 2008;), reminiscent of the 'Orientalist mind-set that shaped European colonialism' (Camilleri, 2008: 11). If Europe is returning to its old civilizing mission by naming and taming the barbarians who threaten those values it has projected as a world standard (Vergès, 2011), it is doing so in protest, as though it were a minority culture under threat, and by drawing up the bridge, by abandoning any old fiction of universal community and equal rights for all (Agier, 2011).

The illiberal presented as liberal is silently sliding European societies towards an authoritarianism from which it will be difficult to return, as we know from the dark moments of their history. In this Europe, intent on confronting an uncertain future by seeing difference as a threat and aiming to recover a past purity, the complexities of a changing European public sphere are reduced to a battle between deserving insiders and disrupting outsiders, between settled traditions and foreign influences. The treatment of very real anxieties and insecurities, shared by majorities and minorities, as the deficiencies of multiculturalism, is to fail to address the issues generating such concern – growing economic and welfare insecurity, falling confidence in a providing future, the stresses of market individualism and a vanishing commons, and escalating natural and social hazard and risk. And not only are causes of social stress and division being left unaddressed, but their cultural consequences are being confronted in an aggressive manner, allowing tropes such as Europe suffering from an 'identity problem' due to excessive immigration and cultural hybridization (Kurth, 2006) to dominate public discourse. It is hardly surprising, therefore, that a widespread belief has grown that the road to future prosperity, peace and security lies in returning Europe to a time of cultural clarity and confidence, with the marginal and foreign kept in place, disciplined in the name of community.

The coupling of a nostalgic politics of identity to an exclusionary politics of collective well-being is sustained by experts and opinion formers, busily projecting the future as catastrophic. The tension noted in the preceding chapter between a 'providential' and 'catastrophic' approach to difference and uncertainty is all too evident in European political culture today. The legacy of the post-war European social state – manifest in the commitment to universal welfare, extensive rights, care for the vulnerable, distributive justice, and comprehensive risk avoidance and insurance – finds itself attacked as an anachronism. Its faith in the future as manageable, and on an inclusive and provisioning basis, is considered by a growing number of states and publics – and not only those on the right – as too permissive towards the sources of danger and too lax for an age of heightened risk.

As the next chapter shows, the emerging rhetoric of security places its emphasis on preparedness and resilience over anticipation and avoidance to tackle the hazardous future, including the risks posed by the stranger. The focus now is on addressing the unknown in a warlike fashion, through detailed monitoring and intervention, aided by elaborate technologies of surveillance and control, clear cartographies of the inside and outside, active engineering of public moods and sentiments, a public culture of emergency, and easy suspension of the rules and standards of democracy in the name of securing communal well-being. While the battles of the catastrophe state with the providential state may vary in intensity and outcome between the neoliberal and social democratic nations in Europe, the aggressive culture of the catastrophe state, with society's full complicity, seems to have become commonplace.

The new demagoguery must be seen in this light, as part and parcel of a new mode of governing the indiscernible future – defending society by restricting it and preparing for the future by waging war against it. Its response to the strange and the alien is total, uncompromising, echoing the darkest moments of intolerance in Europe's modern history. Once again the vulnerable, unfortunate and stigmatized are being cast as the enemy that society as a whole is called to repel, even if this means restricting legal and civil liberties, including of those who come to the aid of the errant stranger (see Fekete, 2009, for evidence across Europe on the criminalization of organizations and networks providing humanitarian aid to migrants and asylum seekers).

Europe with the Stranger

The ill wind sweeping across Europe needs to be recognized, and its implications fully considered. At stake is the choice between a confident openness and hesitant suspiciousness towards the new and unknown. Both stances have prevailed in the history of Europe, the one looking ahead and outwards with curiosity and reciprocity in the name of humanism, cosmopolitanism, progress and democracy, and the other with haughty suspicion and foreboding, sometimes in the name of these very ideals, but jealously guarded for Europe and Europeans. The European heritage is one of both democratic engagement and authoritarian exclusion. With so many global interdependencies shaping the Europe of the twenty-first century, a purist retreat can only be judged counter-historical, a red rag to Europe's sizeable minority and an alienated world majority whose collaboration Europe needs for future peace, stability and economic opportunity. Now home to millions of people from non-European backgrounds, and with its many religious and cultural dispositions, Europe is a crossing of transnational networks that incorporate almost all its citizens and residents. It is as much a space of longings rooted in myths of origin and tradition, as it is a space of cosmopolitan identities and attachments, and hybrid geographies of cultural formation. In such a Europe, it seems anachronistic and potentially incendiary to close the borders, to play the game of good insiders and bad outsiders, to defend ethnic and cultural purity, and to demonize everything alien.

There can be no denying that these are uncertain and turbulent times, with Europe, too, confronted by the vicissitudes of a fast-moving, under-regulated and interdependent world. The concerns of Europeans regarding employment and welfare security, quality of life and future hope, social cohesion and cultural identity, and crime and safety, all periodically highlighted by EU opinion surveys, should not be ignored. Nor should their xenophobic manifestations be dismissed as unreasonable and ridiculous. It will not suffice to expose the error of blaming the stranger for the anxieties felt by Europeans; by showing that migrants and refugees are the victims of poverty and violence, that immigrants bring new capabilities and resources, that Muslims are other than would-be terrorists, or that the causes of risk and insecurity are structural and institutional. The roots of public anxiety that make it easy to scapegoat the stranger need to be tackled head on, through reforms aiming at job generation, fair pay, equal access, universal well-being, equable prospect and shared common life. Only then will the temptation to name the migrant and subaltern as the threat to the prosperity, well-being and cohesion of the many, seem anomalous.

This is a significant task at a time when states and bureaucracies, uncertain and exposed in the face of mounting hazard, rely on inflammatory labelling to allay the fears and anxieties of their publics. However, Europe's legacy of providential, rather than catastrophic, response to hazard and uncertainty – typified by the battles to form the welfare state after the Second World War under similar conditions of adversity – should act as a compass of political reorientation. This cannot be proposed as a recommendation of return, as this would make light of the specificities of time and place. For example, previously, popular interest in the social state was influenced by persuasions of class justice, peaceful coexistence and national prosperity. Instead, the aim of progressive forces in and beyond government should be to recover the provisioning principle as the basis of response to adversity and turbulence, updated to suit the circumstances of today.

A start would be to make cause once again for the plural, open and collective society as the basis of facing the future, by showing the gains to be had – for majorities and minorities and for indigenes and strangers – from a multivocal and democratic public sphere, underwritten by a state that minimizes risk and vulnerability by distributing social capability and ensuring that the commons, however defined, remains protected and valued. At present, there is no credible counter-narrative to the neoliberal/catastrophe doctrine embraced alike by progressives and conservatives, and, as yet, no perception of the escalations of xenophobia as unjust, unnecessary, and a dangerous provocation. In renewing its social democratic/provisioning legacy, Europe needs once again to believe that gender, class and racial and sexual equality remain central to the good society, that universal access to the means of well-being releases new capabilities and reduces envy and resentment, that democracy deepened and extended reinforces social responsibility and resilience, that protection of the collective infrastructure and shared commons strengthens civic culture, and that widespread economic opportunity, parity and security reduce conflict and disaffection.

We can turn to some of these interventions, beginning with the idea of a social Europe, which finds itself decidedly on the back foot in a neoliberal Europe. Until the 1990s, the politics of European integration committed itself to welfare equity to balance the Union's market-driven economic policies. Policies to strengthen regional and agricultural policy, upgrade and harmonize welfare provision, improve workplace democracy, extend human, social and constitutional rights, and step up transnational obligations were vigorously defended as a means of unlocking new creativity, mitigating against the uneven outcomes of market-based competitiveness, and strengthening the social dimension of the 'one Europe' project. The quest for social justice, equity and solidarity, including qualified recognition of the stranger within and beyond Europe, was seen as legitimate and achievable. Into the twenty-first century, however, publics in Europe are presented with a scenario of new global hazards and risks, a faltering and divided European economy, criticism of the EU as too soft or disorganized in the fields of immigration, welfare and security. Thus, the principle of a social Europe finds itself dismissed as anachronistic or unaffordable. Any protest against deepening injustice and inequality, as witnessed in the waves of opposition across Europe to draconian welfare reforms resulting from the current financial crisis, has had little effect on reform even if governments have toppled. It seems that no alternative can be imagined or defended compellingly, and even the practised machinery of the European social model is considered inadequate.

Yet, without the honed collectivist practices of that European social model, there is little to prevent the majorities facing adversity from sliding into xenophobic sentiment towards the stranger who is scapegoated for the difficult circumstances. A Europe of harmonized social protections remains the only basis on which the interests of the many, including those most at risk, can be served.

Protections such as welfare, fiscal and occupational democracy, underwritten by state-guaranteed insurance schemes, can help to temper animosity and envy, and to support a culture of social care and cohesion. Of course, this is not guaranteed, as we know from instances in welfare state history of social expectation without recognition of the other or the commons, as well as situations where the provisions become the focal point of discrimination against the 'undeserving'. But with risk and uncertainty as pronounced as they are now, and with public culture so suspicious of difference and newness, there appears no foundation for Europe to face the future with openness and solidarity, without the guarantees of the social state. A Europe in which publics squabble over collective resources is unlikely to regard the strange and unfamiliar with curiosity and interest.

Prosaic though it may appear, it is necessary to protect and, if anything, extend the European social model, so that the basic needs and prospects of those who find themselves on the shores of Europe are secured without prejudice, through an ethic of responsibility for the communal and marginal that is institutionalized. This means restoring – at national and European level – once familiar measures rendered abnormal by market-led and individualist thinking, underwriting individual and social rights, income and welfare security, social and spatial justice, collective services and spaces, and dignified forms of human integration. Working below the surface, such measures present the communal as capacious, indivisible and shared, in much the same way as we have seen in chapter 3 in relation to the mediation of difference in the urban unconscious. The provisions of the social state too are silent moderators of diversity and difference, pragmatically bridging the gap between the familiar and the unknown, the private and the public, the self and the other.

But a silent commons will not suffice. By the late twentieth century, the social model had become so taken for granted and so detached from the original motivation to tackle want, risk and uncertainty that what it provided ceased to be seen as a means of meeting needs and resolving differences through the commons. Its renewal as a cultural imaginary will require restoration of public commitment to the principle of collective provision and protection without discrimination. This is the prime challenge facing a progressive politics of integration in Europe. To recover the social model by stealth without public endorsement will not suffice, as newly elected social democratic governments have discovered to their cost; nor will hollow declarations of community. Put differently, the anxieties and animosities that sustain the catastrophe model will recede only when public understanding of Europe as a commons changes.

The social model requires cultural validation, if it is to play its role in a politics for the stranger, with the help of appropriate symbolic, affective and practical reinforcements. Many changes are needed, including appreciation by decision-makers and peoples – national and European – of community as a gathering of multiple publics, interests and affiliations, membership as more than a right of birth or naturalization (allowing, for example, recognition based on social contribution), shared spaces and services as a plenitude when kept free from appropriation, and identity formation as a hybrid of the new and old, the human and non-human. Above all, there is a need for the future to be sensed as the unknown negotiated through these kinds of motilities (e.g., public understanding of the plural communal and of border crossing as the means of developing distributed capability and inventiveness born out of cultural experimentalism). In this way, the social model can regain felt legitimacy, giving reason and instinct to reject the machinations of the catastrophe model as unnecessary and anomalous.

At face value, the present may not appear the most opportune time for reinventing public interest in a commons that stands for the stranger too. With Europe as fragmented, anti-collectivist and suspicious of the stranger as it is now, the chances of a provisioning public culture seem slight. Yet the frustrations and disappointments of the catastrophe culture are clearly visible. The current banking crisis, threatening to engulf entire economies and destroy the livelihoods of millions of people for years to come, has yielded little public appetite in mainland Europe for austerity measures or increased corporatist management of the economy, even if governments by choice or under duress continue to profess the unviability of anything different. While the potential of an alternative, socially embedded, economy remains underexplored, a subaltern discourse of public ownership and control, corporate social responsibility, ethical and green enterprise, human-oriented development, and long-term economic planning is finding its way into mainstream policy deliberation and public discussion (Hart, Laville and Cattani, 2010). With sustained political will and momentum in the EU, aided by movements campaigning for the social economy in different European countries, this latent interest could convert into reforms with demonstrable benefits, gradually dismantling the hegemony of austerity/corporatist economics. In contrast to the early years of neoliberal experimentation, which promised market individualism as freedom, there is decreasing public conviction in its measures to tackle risk and uncertainty. The expansionary and social democratic measures introduced by some governments in response to the immediate shocks of the current banking crisis were not rejected by a sceptical public but by vested corporate and ideological interests.

There is no guarantee that any shift towards the provisioning economy will be accompanied by any measure of sympathy for the stranger – as worker, welfare recipient or future entrepreneur. The history of the social model, as already noted, is one of withdrawal from the stranger during times of adversity, and of qualified support at other times. On the other hand, growing social acceptance of a fairer, better-regulated and needs-based economy can only be an opportunity for progressive political forces to demonstrate that the integration of the outsider does not mean loss of opportunity for the insider, but, rather, occasion to unlock new potential, benefit from new alliances and minimize the costs of exclusion. Key to this, is public understanding of the shared turf as a productive sphere when kept open and incomplete. Here, the importance of how Europe, as a still forming and weak commons, is imagined remains of considerable significance.

Thus far, European integration has been projected by opinion makers and politicians as a coming together of already formed entities and legacies, or as a process leading to the completion of a transnational formation with its own political, cultural and institutional fixities. Europe is understood as a community of communities or as a community to come, each already defined in its configuration and orientation. Both as a confederation of national communities and as a post-national arrangement, Europe is seen to be of and for itself, distinct from other political and cultural communities, clear about its past and its destiny. In this envisioning, the claims of the stranger – also understood as pre-formed – can only be judged anomalous, an infringement, a concession. But the projection of Europe, as it might be developed from its multiple cultures and ethnicities, diverse geographies of organization and attachment, and daily crossings and combinations, would present a very different kind of social formation, one, incidentally, far closer to the hybrid that everyday Europe really is. If Europe comes to be felt as a never finished experiment, an undermining of fixed notions of community (Franke, 2005), there is some scope for it to be grasped as a gathering of strangers.

Then a politics of the stranger will no longer seem peculiar, for Europe will be understood as no other than the encounter between strangers and the unfamiliar. Of course, even such a public sphere will not be immune from pressure to yield a hierarchy of strangers. It could simply do what is common today; organize for *some* strangers, and keep down its troublesome subalterns or its migrants and minorities who have arrived from afar (Shehu, 2011; Chambers, 2010). The onus, thus, remains to articulate a politics of the stranger that makes less of provenance and subjectivity and more of the terms and conditions of sharing the commons; veering towards the many, but also organizing for civic participation so that Europe and its identities and obligations emerge out of the encounter (Connolly, 2010). This requires some groundwork, if the vulnerable stranger is to be given a chance. It means extending, rather than restricting, the provisions of the European social state socially and spatially to ensure that the stranger – whoever and wherever in Europe – is treated with dignity. It also means doing more with the diplomatic mode of decision-making that has had to be honed to facilitate the passage of EU policy initiatives through the Union's diverse and frequently warring political constituencies (Amin and Thrift, 2012). Though this mode has not prevented negative consequences for certain strangers (e.g., stepped-up measures against minorities, immigrants and asylum seekers under pressure from nationalist forces), its emphasis on negotiated settlement makes for a more inclusive Europe, assuming the desire for social democratic change can be reinvigorated and given momentum through a new European Constitution or strengthened powers for the EU's elected bodies.

No move towards a Europe for the stranger can rely on institutional legacies alone. Progressive forces in Europe need to make explicit the value of the common resources and civic freedoms enjoyed by the many. A passion for democratic pluralism has to re-emerge, showing that the rights and freedoms enjoyed by the many have frequently originated in battles fought by subjects once considered strangers and subalterns, that there has been no loss as a result of the democratic advances made, but that the rights and freedoms are at risk under the prevailing logic of deserving majorities and usurping minorities. The silent embarrassment that surrounds notions of the open and shared commons has to convert into a felt desire once again. The history of universally accessed public spaces and services, collectively owned assets and multiple occupancy of the public sphere needs to be retold as the history of civic integration, capability formation, active citizenship and communal interest. It must be repeated over and again, in schools, public debate, the media and political arenas, gradually allowing shared concerns to be named, forging communities and collective sentiments and orientations out of occupancy of the commons.

To enchant this vernacular is to re-propose Europe's public spaces and vigorous public sphere, its general rules and rights and communal services, as the means of addressing the challenges posed by an uncertain and turbulent future. It is to look to the commons and to collective endeavour to tackle adversity. It is to sense the value of engaging with the unknown with all available resources and capabilities, and to accept that the way ahead, full of unavoidable risks and uncertainties, is best tackled collectively and democratically. Such a Europe needs the active work of opinion makers, policy communities, politicians and civic forces, campaigning for the social model, exposing the limitations of the catastrophe model, pressing for policies that are fair to the stranger, and claiming for Europe the sentiments of hospitality, mutuality, solidarity and care for the commons (Amin, 2004; Amin and Thrift, 2012). If the momentum is maintained, the brokers of power and opinion may be forced to concede that the stranger must return as an ally in facing the future in an open and peaceful way.

To think of Europe along these lines may seem fanciful given the current lurch towards nationalism and xenophobic Europhilia, as states and societies retreat into familiar zones of affiliation and expectation to ensure their anxieties and needs are addressed. Is it not unrealistic to expect Europe's majorities, turning to their states and nations for an answer, to consider the stranger and a Europe of open endings in these circumstances (Balibar, 2011)? Perhaps: but the incompleteness and subsidiarity of Europe may also turn out to be a strength, a means of adding another layer of address without the xenophobic baggage, if the interests of majorities could be served alongside those of the stranger. Europe, potentially, could make the most of its constitutive pluralism and exteriority (Verstraete, 2010). The EU opinion surveys of majorities anxious about their cultural moorings, material well-being and future security show that these majorities have both xenophobic and liberal leanings. They blame the stranger and the South for their woes, but they also believe Europe – and, by association, themselves – to stand for peace, equality, fairness, freedom of expression and openness to others. This dualism is an opportunity. Assuming the insecurities that feed the fears of Europeans could be tackled through interventions at diverse scales, liberal sentiment could return to recognize the stranger as anything but responsible for the woes of Europe, far from a drain on Europe's resources.

Conclusion

As elsewhere in this book, this chapter has kept clear of a politics of 'befriending the stranger' to tackle the spreading 'global politics of fear' (Dallmayr, 2010: 1) and, once again, out of a lack of conviction in its efficacy. Europe is trapped in a harsh biopolitics of aversion towards the stranger, sustained by a filigree of measures to define, contain, vilify and discipline the anomalous outsider. Appeals to a common humanity or ethic of care will do little to disrupt the machinic power of this biopolitics, or the anxiety and fear that it feeds on, as well as its own use of ethical reasoning to typecast the stranger as uncaring, illiberal, violent, deranged. In addition, because the European public sphere is too thin, but also too quick to coalesce around sentiments that place the rest of the world on the outside in its more active moments, it does not seem appropriate to explore a politics of the stranger located in constitutional patriotism, revival of traditional ideas of Europe, and readings of the European public sphere as a particular set of manners.

Instead, the chapter has looked to Europe as a becoming, an unfinished project, a space of cross-currents irreducible to Europe, in order to think and feel the stranger anew, with the help of an explicit politics of social inclusion and empowerment. A case has been made for social Europe, reinforced at national and EU level and across a spectrum of instituted interventions, as a means of neutralizing anxieties and aversions heightened in turbulent times, legitimating once again the viability and desirability of a system of non-discriminatory social provisions, and restoring credibility in a politics of inclusion and engagement in facing the future. Social Europe has been offered as the counterweight to neoliberalism and racial biopolitics, on the grounds that the leanings and learnings of the commons, when replenished, protected, and daily used, could foster a different attitude towards future risk and uncertainty, one without need for the uses of xenophobia.

But such an achievement, ultimately, is a matter of political will. The renewal and eventual success of democratic mobilization for a plural and open Europe, whether it draws on the civic formations of the commons or not, depends on the intensity of parliamentary and extra-parliamentary interest in the political composition and openness of the EU, in the tone of political and public rhetoric on Europe and its public reception, in the balance of power between diverse national and European spheres of influence, and in the policies and arguments adopted by the institutions of Europe. Success depends on finding the appropriate political force and organization. While this chapter has named the principles of a provisioning in Europe, it has not named the actors – the movements, parties, governments and other bodies – that would secure its progress. This is partly because no coalition is obvious at the moment, and also because the actors are most likely to appear once momentum builds in the public arena behind some of the principles. But to be so much at the beginning of a provisioning Europe is also a sign of considerable fragility, for, as the next chapter shows, the gains of catastrophism are more advanced, and its allies stronger.

− 6 −

A Calamitous End?

When the body of the enemy can no longer be liquidated with direct assault, the possibility presents itself to the attacker of making his existence impossible, by immersing the enemy in an unliveable milieu.

Sloterdijk, 2009: 44

We must transform not only our armed forces but also the Department that serves them by encouraging a culture of creativity and intelligent risk-taking. We must promote a more entrepreneurial approach to developing military capabilities, one that encourages people, all people, to be proactive and not reactive, to behave somewhat less like the bureaucrats and more like venture capitalists.

Donald Rumsfeld, 2002; cited in O'Malley, 2010: 501[1]

Introduction

If this book has ventured a politics of hope, it has done so aware of the contingencies of context. To acknowledge the creative possibilities of situated practice is to recognize

[1]Reprinted by permission of the publisher (Taylor & Francis Ltd, http://www.tandfonline.com).

also their instability and the need to work at keeping them in place to survive the challenge of other orderings. It is not possible to remain unaware of the weight that bears down on a politics of togetherness in the contemporary Western calculus of community, as we have seen in the discussion on the remainders of race and on the contagions of xenophobia in Europe. The incursions of an organized geopolitics of aversion towards subalterns and an informal biopolitics of suspicion of stigmatized bodies in the encounter between strangers are deep. Indeed, it may be difficult to avoid such a future, as the situation is poised to get worse, with a state-endorsed narrative of the future as continually perilous and increasingly out of control takes hold, proposing aggressive interventions in the order of things – including the potentialities of the stranger – to protect those societies considered prone to repeated major assaults.

It is this calamitous prognosis and its preparations that inform this sober last chapter, which engages with a new apocalyptic imagination coursing through Anglo-American public culture. This is an imaginary that, by design or default, draws a parallel between diverse threats such as global warming, health pandemics, natural catastrophes, technological risks, and international crime and terrorism, seeing them as the perturbations of a world system on the edge of breakdown or, at least, one so complex and interconnected that it continuously generates new and escalating risks. The recurrence, spread, severity and mutability of the world's natural and social hazards are considered as symptomatic of this state, and its latent conditions are understood to be too volatile or random and non-linear to permit accurate prediction and evasive action. In the apocalyptic imaginary, hazard and risk erupt as unanticipated emergencies, disarming in every manifestation and in every way.

This is the gist of a dizzying portrayal in many contemporary novels, films, reports, media broadcasts, and scientific and policy forecasts of the not too distant future, prophesying a string of catastrophes that threaten the end of life as known. In these projections, the word 'if' is displaced by the word 'when', accompanied by graphic details of the shape of things to come, verifications by various tools – tested and invented – of calculation, and memorable summaries of the future (e.g., the thunder of the four horsemen of the Apocalypse wreaking destruction in the West in Žižek's book *Living in the End Times*). The world architecture that Sloterdijk (2005) has described as a foam-like structure, just about protecting life in each of its bubbles but also pushing in on it and altering its morphology, is about to collapse, with its fragile atmospheres of breathability punctured, in these portrayals of an intertwined planet at risk.

The forecasts of the new catastrophism are far from proven or accepted, assured though they may sound. As the controversies on climate change show, the calamitous warnings, once in the public arena, step into a battleground of competing truths, proofs and interests, having to work hard to make their case heard and accepted (Pearce, 2010; Szerszynski and Urry, 2010). They stimulate counter-narratives and counter-proposals. In turn, eventual outcomes follow no script, but are melded by complex latencies and contingencies that defy even the most sophisticated forecasting models. All this said, the language of catastrophism is bedding in a powerful guide to thought and action, shaping decisions taken by governments and other corporate actors as well as public and expert understanding of the knowable and actionable world. The return of apocalyptic thinking is acting as a foreclosure to imagination, a template for behaviour and a structure of feeling. This is why its diagnosis and proposals cannot be ignored.

This chapter focuses on the political work being done by new principles of risk management that are accompanying the new thinking. It examines the ambiguities of a new rhetoric of preparedness and resilience (replacing one of avoidance and insurance), on the one hand, proposing draconian interventions to alter the conditions of emergence, but also, on the other hand, expecting greater social effort to spread responsibility in coping with uncertainty and adversity. While one seeks to restrict freedom in order to strike at the sources of hazard and risk, the other expects citizens to play their part in the security state. The chapter considers the implications of both moves for the stranger considered as threat. The prospect outlined is bleak, but it is also suggested that exposure of the harms of draconian intervention, accompanied by a vigorous politics of caution and precaution, could make way for a more modest and more democratic politics of emergency.

From Protection to Preparedness

After the devastating experience of the two world wars, and the threat of total annihilation presented by the nuclear escalations of the Cold War, the comprehensive securitization of national borders and peoples became a major concern of Western governments in the second half of the twentieth century. A consensus emerged that there could be no repetition of the scale and duration of the damage experienced, when the battle of supremacy between a capitalist West and a communist East could end in annihilation because of the technologies involved and the expansionary imperatives of both sides. During the decades prior to the collapse of communism, and following the global expansion of neoliberalism after the 1980s, Western governments played on the ambivalence of simultaneously suspending and aggravating war in the name of peace and prosperity at home by committing to national welfare security and to the aggressive defence of the realm. Whatever the meanderings of preparing for social and military security, the common underlying assumption was that the future could be made safe by controlling it.

Two important premises of national security came to the fore in the early post-war period. The first was an awareness that the profligacy of wartime mass-destruction technological experiments (with chemicals, biological agents and nuclear weapons) needed to be checked. An anxiety of unforeseen horror grew, underwritten by various international accords, heightened public concern, and political awareness of the consequences of further technological proliferation. While concerns fell short of halting experimentation, they sought to place developments such as the build up of a nuclear arsenal within a frame of fighting known enemies in a known theatre of war (fuelling, in turn, national economic recovery and competitiveness through the growth of the military-industrial complex). Military and other forms of risk came to be understood as avoidable or winnable, on the assumption that the probabilities were calculable, and the risks avoidable – the second premise of securitization. The belief spread that a cadre of experts – scientists, statisticians, strategists, forecasters, officials and politicians – could be entrusted to 'foresee, and keep from materializing, new dangers on the horizon' (Jasanoff, 2010: 18).

Such premises produced a distinctive culture of risk management, based on assurances of prediction, planning and insurance, to map uncertainty as legible and governable. The period perfected the tools of anticipation based on actuarial tabulations of recurrent bad events in the past, in order to calculate the timing, location and scale of likely future hazards. While decision-makers were anything but complacent regarding the arts of foresight, they convinced themselves and their publics that a robust science of calculation, backed by effective central planning and responsiveness, allowed them to prepare for the future by hedging off the threat or minimizing the damage caused by it. Accordingly, the preparation and implementation of detailed plans against want, attack, disease and adversity became a major preoccupation, with responsibility placed in the hands of experts and central authorities, accompanied by effort to construct or enrol an obeying public.

In the affairs of warfare, this meant building vast military capability, elaborate defence strategies and demonstrable intent, so as to forestall or vanquish attack. It also meant producing a trusting and compliant public with the help of various forms of propaganda and civil defence exercises, including far-fetched practices such as vigils in high places to spot incoming missiles or ducking under desks to survive a nuclear attack (Thompson, 1980; Collier and Lakoff, 2008). Similarly, planning for welfare security involved the roll out of free or affordable state provisions across the spectrum of social need in order to build individual and collective resilience against future adversity, once again propped up by a culture of belief in the national welfare state as a system of risk minimization. The stance towards dangers that still managed to get through was one of full recompense from an insurance industry confident of its ability to underwrite the future out of the differential between accumulated premiums and past payout trends held to evolve in a predictable manner.

The calculus of risk – confronted by pronounced escalation in the frequency, scale and unpredictability of hazard – has changed, enough to invalidate the post-war legacy of anticipation and insurance. A sense has grown that while the causes might be known of the floods, hurricanes, droughts, violent acts, pandemics, human displacements, incursions and economic meltdowns that repeatedly assail a growing number of regions, their timing, magnitude and spatial coordinates remain elusive. Increasingly, hazards and risks are apprehended just before or just after the event, whose mutations and contagions make anticipation and planning all that more difficult, an inexact science. The arrival of the recurring but always different catastrophic event in a West used to being protected from sudden and severe harms, seeing them confined to the desperate and volatile regions of the world, has thrown into doubt the validity and efficacy of the tried machinery of risk anticipation and management. And this, at various levels, including reduced public confidence in the validations of science, expertise and central authorization,

heightened public debate on risk society and its consequences, institutional doubt over the viability and efficacy
of universal provisions and protections, concern among
strategists and decision-makers over the limitations of
actuarial calculation or linear projection and associated
technologies of anticipation and avoidance, and reticence
in the insurance industry to underwrite the future in anything other than minimalist and selective ways.

In these circumstances of heightened uncertainty about
the mechanics of the future and how best to exercise lever-
age, the certitudes of risk management have evaporated,
replaced by provisional arrangements often lacking the
wisdom of considered opinion or the benefit of accumulated evidence, and inevitably influenced by mainstreams
of circulating opinion. These range from weary resignation
or disbelief in the idea of an unmanageable future and
laissez-faire (propped up by a neoliberal culture of indi-
viduated response to risk), to stepped-up collective responsibility and developing new tools to illuminate obscure
potentialities. Despite these differences, the foundations of
a distinctively new technoculture of risk management seem
to be falling into place.

One innovation is the adoption of probabilistic tools of
risk appraisal, which are considered better suited to
mapping unstable environments evolving in non-linear
ways and through complex interactions. Actuarial calculation, based on the projection of past trends and events, is
giving way to mathematical simulation of the future on a
'what if' rather than 'when' basis. The calculations are not
linear or evolutionary projections, but sophisticated com-
putations of probability, simulations of likely scenarios
based on processing large volumes of data through software models that seek to replicate real-life parametric
conditions and possibilities. The yield of these attempts to
model randomness, parametric change, emergence, and in
general the living ecology, is a menu of likely possibilities
under different conditions. While the designers and opera-
tives of probabilistic modelling recommend judicious

interpretation of the scenarios, fully aware of the inaccuracy and uncertainty built into the very architecture of the models, the policymakers and practitioners, pressed to get things right under the weight of public expectation and circumstance, are finding it hard to abandon habits based on actuarial calculation, which include the inclination to treat scenarios as predictions and to act as though the event can be anticipated. The 'Climategate' controversy, with its extraordinary public exposure of the methods and protagonists of research on global warming and of the interests at stake behind diverse truth claims (Pearce, 2010), is emblematic of the growing disjuncture between a science of risk, adapting to make sense of highly turbulent complex systems, and practitioners and publics troubled by scientific ambiguity and policy incertitude.

While these controversies of future anticipation continue to rage, the assumption that society can be fully protected weakens by the day (in degrees dependent on the strength of commitment of states to the legacy of comprehensive protections). Facing the pressure of rising public expectations, escalating costs and mounting adversity, governments find themselves walking a fine line between assuring citizens and corporations that their future remains secure and in safe hands, and preparing them for times whose turbulence and volatility defy anticipation and prevention. This is especially so in a context in which publics are more informed and sceptical, but also more demanding of the authorities than ever before. Thus, on the one hand, hazard and risk are being understood as unavoidable, best tackled through strategies of minimization and mitigation, rather than those of pre-emption and avoidance. Public authorities, security organizations and insurers are beginning to accept that, even if the probabilities can be calculated, the unrelenting recurrence of harmful events – terrorist attacks, floods, landslides, health epidemics, wild economic swings – proves that they can do only so much. Out of this acceptance is coalescing the opinion that the central authorities can help to limit the damage and aid recovery, along with building the means of future resilience. But it cautions against expecting much more than this.

On the other hand, authorities are conscious that they cannot ignore the expectations of a public used to being shielded from mass calamity, believing the West to be a better and safer place than elsewhere, and relying on delegated institutions to secure the state. They realize that the emerging culture of risk management has to be perceived as fit for purpose, which means reworking public understanding concerning the best way of securitizing an uncertain future. One response is the invention of new modes of justification, to borrow from Boltanski and Thévenot (2006), with the help of keywords that can become shorthand for new ways of thinking and acting upon risk. One keyword is 'resilience', extracted from the obscurities of scholarship on self-correcting natural and physical systems, but now a commonplace of risk management signalling the virtue of distributing the capacity to withstand and recover from hazard. Intended to strengthen anticipatory capability and social responsiveness during and after an event, 'resilience' signals a desire to shift away from the idea of the protected society towards that of the self-defending society, in which citizens and civic bodies reappear as interceptors, knowledge brokers and architects of reconstruction. It conjectures that a risk environment marked by frequent and localized surprises requires responsibility to be shared between a central authority that leads on strategy, foresight and securitizing the essentials of survival (from protecting the realm to ensuring capital accumulation and access to resources), and a civil society that looks out for danger and gets involved in protecting itself.

Accordingly, cloaked in the language of resilience, every step taken by states to round up the suspicious, research new mass vaccines, build barrages and defence shields, capitalize markets or secure borders, is accompanied by public campaigns to dampen expectation, explain the end of the age of comprehensive security and insurance, and propose that the crisis-prone future can be managed through a new division of labour. In what appears to be a decisive shift from a command-and-control model to a strategic partnership model, the governance of risk is becoming explicitly politicized and publicly referenced (Jasanoff, 2010). Any pretence of managing the future from a central bureaucracy, in the way imagined in the second half of the twentieth century, is melting away. Tackling risk, itself understood as a multiple entity, is presented as not only a matter of choosing the right measures, but also a matter of changing perceptions and expectations about the future. Tackling risk is posed as a challenge of reworking futurity, creating and handling controversies, managing expectations and fears, mobilizing plural knowledge and effort, and naturalizing new practices of mitigation such as pre-emption, precaution and preparedness (Anderson, 2010). The governance of risk, one could say, is becoming a battle of imaginaries and persuasions in an effort by officials to present the shortcomings of the new model as manageable.

The Politics of Preparedness

What is the result of this reframing of the future as apocalyptic and in need of emergency measures, of perceiving the world as full of peril? Is this a warning to step back from the abyss by altering ways of living (Olsson, 2007)? Is it a way of exhibiting the disastrous world and its consequences as a normal feature of the contemporary West (Ekström, 2011)? What is to be made of the emerging culture of risk management? Should the transition from a culture of total protection and risk avoidance to one of joint responsibility and risk mitigation be considered a democratic opening – an opportunity to bridge difference and to mobilize all available resources to confront radical uncertainty? Or does it come with uneven protections and an imbalance of power, as the 'strategic' role of a central authority comes to include warlike preparations against known and unknown enemies in the name of protecting the nation (Diprose et. al., 2008)?

Preparedness as shared responsibility

The potential for democratization cannot be denied, even if its source is a central authority stretched and exhausted by a changing risk environment. Whatever the cause, the opportunity itself to decentre power and initiative might be considered as reason enough, all the more if the process of harnessing the effort of diverse actors becomes an effective way of unlocking collective learning, local responsiveness and resilience capacity. Perhaps necessity is finally creating the change in practice long advocated by experts in science and technology studies, as well as in disaster studies, working on decision-making in uncertain or turbulent environments, for a better division of labour between expert and lay communities. Let us consider two important contributions, one from each field, to test this proposition.

In *Acting in an Uncertain World*, which examines major late twentieth-century controversies in France such as the handling of nuclear waste disposal, BSE, and muscular dystrophy, Callon, Lascoumes and Barthe (2009) conclude decidedly against the state-driven tradition of decision-making. Centrism, with its emphasis on the deciding state, hierarchical expertise and closed circuits, is judged to be both undemocratic and ineffective: too cumbersome and too remote to be able to follow the developments and surprises of risk society, too opaque to carry a sceptical and knowledgeable public, and too rule-bound to yield informed or always sensible decisions. The book proposes an alternative approach to risk management in a world characterized by both distributed know-how and exposure to complex technological interdependencies and multiple sources of hazard. Drawing on diverse case studies, but especially on evidence from the field of muscular dystrophy, where slow advancement from the traditional centres of authority has led to productive collaborations between the medical industry, patient groups, professionals and researchers that have forced change in care practice, this book proposes a way forward based on shared knowledge and responsibility.

Callon, Lascoumes and Barthe reject the plausibility of an all-seeing and acting authority and, with this, any notion of a lasting fix. Instead, recognizing that solutions need to be renewed and renegotiated as circumstances and knowledge evolve, they suggest a procedure able to convert potential risks into matters of common concern and objects of public and political controversy, so that awareness comes to be shared, and decisions subjected to the jostle of competing perspectives and interests. Outcome is related to the validity of procedure, the legitimacy of the vision of experts alone put into question. While the authors stop short of considering whether their proposal to rely on distributed and publicly validated authority would work in all situations of risk, including emergencies of war, sabotage or infrastructural collapse that demand instantaneous response (Amin, 2011), they leave us in little doubt that the politics of the turbulent unknown requires more, rather than less, democracy. This conclusion is echoed elsewhere in science studies, for example, Sheila Jasanoff's (2010) plea for risk models to be developed as 'technologies of humility' that explicitly factor into their forecasts the knowledge that hazards tend to affect the vulnerable first and most severely. Others also interested in the biases of calculative practice suggest rethinking scenario-planning as more of a choice between preferred worlds than as a projection or protection of the status quo, open to the persuasions of alternative forecasting methods such as modelling based on open-source or do-it-yourself technologies (cf. Sardar, 2010).

The second case for distributed action originates in research on disasters, which frequently remarks on the qualities of human resilience and organization during a crisis. An important recent contribution is Rebecca Solnit's (2009) study of major disasters in Europe and North America over the last 100 years, a book that leans unequivocally towards grass-root capability. Solnit claims that during the earthquakes in San Francisco in 1906 and Mexico City in 1985, the Blitz and 7/7 in London, and the 9/11 attacks in New York, social inventiveness, altruism and solidarity came quickly to the fore after a first moment of shock and disorientation. She argues that this occurred especially when the central authorities found themselves overwhelmed, either forced or prepared to give ground, which allowed communities of care and reconstruction to form and speed up recovery (and in a fairer way), thanks to the release of collective initiative and resource.

Contradicting expectations that fear the worst from humans in conditions of chaos and disorder, these disasters are cited as having avoided any surge in feral, selfish or apathetic behaviour. Solnit finds that people quickly formed into groups that attended to the well-being of the weak and the vulnerable, working with each other to secure the interests of the community at large. Strangers under duress became collaborators. In stark contrast, disasters like Katrina in New Orleans, overrun by hysterical media reports and heavy-handed authorities, are held to have yielded a slow and exclusionary recovery process that excluded the weak and vulnerable, worked only for those with means, and removed any sense of the collective commons. Solnit traces the problem to the relationship between the central authorities and citizens. Here, claims Solnit, in the gap between popular initiative quashed or corrupted by hierarchical power, and delegated authorities and opinion makers reduced to panic measures, needs were compromised, capacities underutilized and responsibility abrogated. Strangers under duress became enemies or indifferent subjects.

Solnit's book is a manifesto for self-organization, even in the most difficult circumstances. Its claims arise out of a combination of historical observation, anarchist belief and the supposition, following William James (2003), that open and plural systems prove to be resilient when their compositional multiplicity is given free reign. Unhindered interaction in a plural ecology – random individually but checked collectively – is held to enable recovery from perturbations that threaten to tip the system into chaos. While such thinking remains inconclusive about the ability of self-regulating systems to prevent tipping points without organized forms of emergency management (O'Riordan and Lenton, 2011), it returns rule by numbers into the centre of discussion on managing unstable systems. In James's case, it seems that first-hand experience of one event – the fervent human endeavour he witnessed in the immediate aftermath of the 1906 San Francisco earthquake – reinforced his thinking on the value of pluralism.

Here we have two compelling – and in many ways reassuring – demystifications of catastrophism, concluding in favour of distributed power as both antidote to actions that court disaster and as the means of ensuring balanced recovery from a crisis. In democratic pluralism, they find a better way of organizing for a turbulent and uncertain future. They put catastrophism and its discourse of calamitous preparations, disposable subjects and withdrawn protections in place. For a book such as this one, arguing for a politics of the stranger, they are invaluable allies. Yet a neglect of certain orderings of the contemporary world blunts their case.

Solnit's eulogy to distributed social power rests on a romance of lay knowledge and human altruism and resistance that underestimates the centrality of non-humans – visible and invisible – in ordering (and disrupting) modern life. Large and distributed human settlements rely on extensive management, coordination and interaction, much of this in the hands of non-humans. Without this, there is no intelligence, maintenance or recovery, and all the more so in an age that is constitutively technological, bureaucratized and informational. The heart of modern social formations, as amply recognized by science and technology studies (above all the work of Callon), is an assemblage of interacting humans and non-humans processing vast quantities of data and intelligence to hold things together, to ensure functionality.

The balance between order and disorder rests on the machinic qualities of this assemblage, worked deep into its technological, institutional and infrastructural arrangements. It is no coincidence, for example, that as the interactive intelligence of this assemblage expands due to the digitalization of information and its subsequent governance by software, so too does its centrality in the jostles of power and control. At the most dramatic end, the wars of states and terrorists are increasingly becoming wars of infrastructure: software- and hardware-aided interventions targeted at other software- and hardware-aided installations. The contemporary turn towards the urbanization of warfare (Graham, 2010) is symptomatic, looking to take out not only concentrated human life, but also the means of intelligence and resilience that sustain life within large conurbations, and the national and global networks they sustain (Sassen, 2010).

While it may well be true that human altruism kicks in after a disaster – perhaps precisely because the hidden machinery of social organization has been incapacitated – the significance of the parts that remain intact should not be underestimated (e.g., radio communications after the 2011 Japanese tsunami, software systems that linked up emergency services in London on 7/7, the disciplinary drills of the New York firemen on 9/11, the materials of rudimentary sanitation in the contaminated city – cf. McFarlane, 2010). It is also worth remembering, as many disaster studies show, that human energy and solidarity dissipate rapidly if help is not felt to be at hand. It may well turn out that the thread separating hopeful cooperation from feral degeneracy lies in the hidden hand of organization and provision, in the automaticity of infrastructures of maintenance and repair that hum in the background to prevent disorder during normal and abnormal times (Graham and Thrift, 2007). In a disaster-prone world, therefore, the efficacy with which the architecture of the mundane is maintained by the hybrid intelligences of central authorities, modellers, connectors, engineers, emergency services, and more, may be much more central than humanist belief acknowledges, as the true measure of resilience.

Preparedness as ontological war

Thought that envisions a balanced division of labour between state and civil society to tackle the turbulent future tends also to ignore the import of state discourse itself commending partnership. A thin line between co-optation and cooperation is crossed when states, as they are doing in the Anglo-American world, introduce disaster management drills in primary schools, condone vigilantism on the street in the war against terror, praise citizens who show initiative in an emergency while disapproving of those who await help, and promote various kinds of bodily enhancements to engineer the resilient subject. Work on the political culture of catastrophism, much of it inspired by Foucault (2003, 2004), remains wary of the deeper implications behind contemporary responses to emergencies calling for the full involvement of the society. The claim here is that the process – now collaborative and distributed – is part of a new governmentality towards the uncertain future, involving interventions with far from benign implications. Civic involvement and civic energy are seen as being drawn into a war of the authorities against the sources of uncertainty and turbulence, including purposefully named foreign entities.

If the post-war security culture pretended it could eliminate risk by declaring war on its perpetrators, the new culture of emergency management, marshalling all available means, intervenes in the conditions of emergence.

This is how critical thought on the West's war on terror interprets the proliferation of pre-emptive strikes, acts of surveillance, erasure and encampment, discourses of good and bad peoples and places; interventions justified by detailed calculations of projected risk, and visualization of horrors to come in the absence of such incursions. These are efforts, as de Goede and Randalls (2009) put it, to clear the way in order to stay ahead in a closely monitored hazardous landscape, a principle of anticipation gradually rolled out to other domains of life. Thus it enjoins implausible and expensive geo-engineering projects to change the chemical composition of the atmosphere or tap new aquifers in order to stave off the effects of global warming, search for psychotropic and biotechnical solutions to sharpen human wit and muscle in adversity, and planning for 'antibiotics and vaccines against infectious diseases *that have not yet emerged*' (Cooper, 2008: 91; original emphasis).

Brian Massumi (2009) describes such interventions as exercises of 'ontopower', in their attempt to rework subjectivities and conditions of existence, counter-mimic the event, and standardize the rules of civic, military and environmental defence. If the social resilience model prepares for recovery after the disaster, and the technologies of humility model for anticipatory reasoning, catastrophism – beckoning all possible allies – is said to intervene in the environment of life itself in order to alter the composition and distribution of harms (Amoore and Hall, 2009). In this attempt to get close to the ground of emergence in a turbulent environment, a telling act of clearance of accumulated social practices and settlements is the exploitation of openings enabled by the informatics and biotechnology revolutions in the war on hazard and risk.

The fast-developing sciences of genetic manipulation, cellular recomposition, pharmacological reconstruction, technological implantation, unlimited cybernetic capability, ubiquitous artificial life, and more, are judged as incursions that make life more knowable than ever before, thus available for redesign. The state is held to be no innocent bystander in these trials, especially when it finds in them the potential to build anticipatory and attacking capability. Melinda Cooper (2008) has argued this in relation to state-led entanglements, begun by the Bush regime, between molecular research, speculative finance and the war on terror. She claims that, facing a landscape considered volatile and experimental, the US state has invested heavily in life-science research aspiring to develop more resilient human and natural life, simultaneously pursuing aggressive deregulation to allow new markets and speculative finance to emerge, and facilitating the exploration of war technologies from the resulting opportunities. The 'institutional conflation of security and public health research, military strategy, environmental politics, and the innovation economy ... *in the name of life in its biospheric dimension, incorporating meteorology, epidemiology, and the evolution of all forms of life, from the microbe* up' (p. 98; emphasis in original), has not been innocent. Research, state, industry and the armed forces have actively collaborated, according to Cooper, resulting in an elite culture which, by design or association, assumes that preparing for a turbulent future means altering the composition of life and then riding on the opportunities presented.

Dillon and Reid (2009) interpret such ontological interventions as a new twist in the liberal way of war: market oriented and entrepreneurial, perceived as encouraging liberal freedom and human potentiality, justifying war as peace and the protection of liberal democracy. And, by diffusion, such liberalism can spread to other areas of defence against adversity. As Fassin and Pandolfi (2010: 10) observe, 'disasters and conflicts are now embedded in the same logic of intervention, which rests on two fundamental elements: the temporality of emergency, which is used to justify a state exception, and the conflation of the political and moral registers manifested in the realization of operations that are at once military and humanitarian'.

Depending on the severity of the stakes and the complicity of publics and elites, the approach noted below by Sloterdijk (2010) in the 'war on terror' can thus spread, to underwrite capital accumulation, manage all kinds of disaster, silence the opponents of technological experimentation and demonize exponents of the cosmopolitan and fully democratic society, all in the spirit of defending the liberal way of life:

> The 'war on terror' possesses the ideal quality of not being able to be won – and thus never having to be ended. These prospects suggest that the postdemocratic trends will enjoy a long life. They create the preconditions with which democratically elected leaders can get away with presenting themselves as commanders in chief. If political thinking limits itself to advising the commander in chief, concepts such as democracy and independent judiciary cultures are only chips in a strategic game. (p. 219)

The transition to this kind of culture of risk management is far from uniform. It is dependent upon the remaining strength of the providential model in different operational and national contexts, along with the strength of public and political opposition to catastrophism. Thus, for example, the approach to climate change, unexpected natural disasters and global pandemics continues to veer more towards caution, deliberation and diplomacy than it does in relation to the war on terror, rogue states and cultural difference. And there remain clear differences between states, based on their security, public and political cultures, with both the UK and USA at the forefront of the aggressive and socially selective attack on the future. Even in the war on terror, as Lentzos and Rose (2009) reveal in their comparative study of policy response to the threat of biological warfare, while the UK has travelled far down the road of catastrophism, planning for community resilience and recovery after the event, France remains committed to the principle of contingency planning, assuming that attack can be anticipated, while

Germany continues to cleave to the post-war legacy of comprehensive state responsibility for protecting the realm. These differences are differences of public expectation and state appraisal of the relative merits of the providential and catastrophic models in dealing with an uncertain future.

Such differences will persist and, with them, the possibility of tempering the excesses of catastrophism, including the abuses of democracy. However, the risk remains that the automaticity of alterations in the fabric of life will shift the calculus of response to the future unknown, and eventually squeeze out the premises of the social state. And then, in the urgency of the moment, the differences between militarism and humanitarianism, between laissez-faire and interventionism, and between democracy and autocracy, will be lost, as the most aggressive states lean on their more measured allies to respond to the hazardous world more selectively and more forcefully, in the name of preserving a threatened liberal way of life.

Catastrophism works on a subjectivity ready to ride the storm, sure of survival, convinced that the balance of force can be shifted to ensure a new habitable dawn (at least until the next emergency). Recent years have seen a considerable escalation of training and awareness exercises by corporations and organizations, as well as states and social groups, to better manage hazard and risk. The evidence suggests a convergence of practice in military, business, professional and life-course training, one increasingly focused on fashioning the entrepreneurial subject. It speaks of soldiers, employees, businesses, leaders and professionals trained to find opportunity in adversity, courage in danger and uncertainty, adaptability and inventiveness in contingency, with victory against a stealthy enemy by getting the habits of the field right. It uncovers a raft of experiments to engineer the physical, psychological and emotional characteristics necessary for a 'new kind of "warrior" subject, more entrepreneurial, flexible and adaptive, more relational and active than is consistent with subjects distinguished by fortitude alone' (O'Malley, 2010: 502). It discovers costly investment in exercises – simulated and real – to create an army of subjects who will remain 'adaptable, intuitive, innovative, independent, skilled, confident and optimistic' (ibid.: 503) in the face of adversity, so as to trade on risk and convert uncertainty into advantage.

The spirit of capitalism is being invoked once again to make capital by finding new opportunity in turbulence (Anderson, 2012). Catastrophism expects its subjects to do no less than mount the horses of the Apocalypse, in the venture capitalist sponsoring the risky idea, the banks and corporations investing in hazard and hazardous times, the soldiers thriving on danger, the states, militias and humanitarian agencies stepping into the war zone, the regulatory agencies daring to push through a drug to combat a biosecurity threat, the gaming teenagers learning to be fearless and adventurous by gaming on screen, and the politicians daring to build the next nuclear reactor. The hyperbole of such adventurism is all too easy to ridicule, and of little help to worn-out populations living close to hazards and reliant on others or their own limited resources to live with adversity in a cautious and restrained way. But it would be an error to dismiss it as a supremacist fantasy that died out with the Bush/Rumsfeld regime, for it is peddled as a narrative of survival by powerful forces able to occlude and discard other alternatives, riding on the affective thrust in contemporary capitalism to mimic the excitable subject. This appears to be the temperament spreading across a variegated landscape, silently denaturalizing a subjectivity of collective provisioning.

Nigel Thrift (2011), noting the corporate labour behind this kind of development, has coined the phrase 'Lifeworld Inc.' to highlight the habit of constantly scanning the environment to stake out a claim. In Lifeworld Inc., 'subjectivity has been turned inside out. In contrast to the idea of the romantic subject with a deep inner core, we now find subjects being built who rely on the onflow of information

in motion to comprehend their place in the world . . .
enmeshed in a web of markings which define their existence, which brand them as them: search engines, social
networking sites, web pages, video clips, ring tones and
mixes, and maps' (p. 16). Lifeworld Inc. subjects are
described to exist in a state of both 'calculated excitation'
and 'paranoiac vigilance', snared by the offerings and
seductions of a 'security-entertainment' complex, claimed
by Thrift to have replaced the 'military-industrial' complex
as the driving force of capitalism. The corporate complex
trading on extreme sports, video games, theatrical citizenship, virtual war simulations, consumer spectacle, speculative behaviour, and other forms of energetic ways of being
in the world that involve extreme emotions, is seen to be
engineering the gladiatorial consumer habituated to the
idea of the future as permanently risky but also apprehended through enthusiastic forms of dwelling.

The pretensions of Lifeworld Inc. are easy to expose as
a corporate gimmick of little interest to subjects unim-
pressed by the thrall of excitable living or disarmed by the
force of an unfolding disaster. But if Lifeworld Inc. is
reason for states, corporations, experts and elites to pull
back from a culture of collective provisions and protections, the figure of the excitable subject – consuming,
associating or warmongering in much the same way – will
be forced into the frontline of defence against escalating
risk and uncertainty, regardless of whether there are many
takers. To see such a reordering of the landscape of survival as a neoliberal delusion that the old world can mock
and reject, is to underrate the power and reach of the
security-entertainment complex. This complex is here to
stay, for much hangs on it, from the viability of a new
phase of capitalist expansion to the security of exposed
populations, both depending on new practices of environmental adjustment to negotiate a probabilistic, uninsurable
and decentred future.

To dismiss catastrophism – its rhetoric, calculus, emotional preparations and tools of intervention – is also to

misjudge the power of argument that presents the future as a string of emergencies. Life, here or there, imagined as a lurch from one testing event to another, forecloses any obligation to know the in-between as well as the processes that explain the event. The event alone is projected to count; its calamities, its humanitarian, infrastructural and environmental costs, its heroes, victims and perpetrators, its relief effort and management needs, all kept in play as the measure of the next event. As a consequence, the everyday continuities and improvisations that precede or follow the event, the processes of 'catastrophization' (Ophir, 2010) that explain and locate the event, disappear from view, no longer considered worthy of attention. The symptom becomes all, and emergency management the norm. From the same analytical zone, thus, stem the interpretation of the tragic event witnessed from afar as reason to reach for humanitarian aid, and of the impending threat closer to home as reason to unleash all available violence on the bearers of the threat.

Catastrophism, now with the complicity of civic society, enrols all available opportunities, including technologies of humility and the expertise and capabilities of diverse knowledge communities. The democratic gestures unwittingly become allies of the security state, tasked to pick up the pieces after the strike that could not be anticipated, used by the state to gather intelligence and prepare society for the worst. This is not to diminish the value of measured and democratic response in response to risk and uncertainty. It is simply to warn of the totalizing intentions of catastrophism. Preparedness as ontological war clears the ground, including the suspension or extension of democracy, craving full support of the society that must be defended. The culture of calamity reorders the world, gives reason to impose new rules on the unruly and the out of joint, change the standards of governing life, and re-establish hierarchies. It has a long history, from the colonial clearances it enabled during the Great Irish famine (Nally, 2011), to more contemporary uses to shock the world into market discipline (Klein, 2008) or to legitimate American adventurism after 9/11 (Rozario, 2007). The stranger, here, only returns as errant, destructive. As Ophir (2011: 3) notes, 'power is entangled with disaster' in all kinds of ways: 'when major threats are anticipated and aid and relief are distributed and administered, disasters are always already politicized'. Generating disaster and administering relief have 'become major ways of governing large populations and dealing with multitudes' and, ever more today, 'catastrophes, even when they are unpredictable and unplanned seem to open opportunities . . . to put disaster to work for stronger political players at the expense of the weaker ones, and to do so in more or planned and orchestrated ways' (ibid.).

Conclusion

Melinda Cooper (2008) pointedly asks what 'becomes of an anti-war politics when the sphere of military action infiltrates the "grey areas" of everyday life, contaminating our "quality of life" at the most elemental level' (p. 98). She suggests that salvaging a politics of peace based on securitizing human well-being in order to push back at the credo of security-as-war will not suffice. Such a politics, even if it can muster the necessary interest and momentum, is considered to miss the ontological changes on which the politics of militarism feeds. For Cooper, another form of counter-mimicry is required:

> In the face of a politics that prefers to work in the speculative mode, what is called for is something like a creative sabotage of the future; a pragmatics of preemptive resistance capable of actualizing the future outside of the police-able boundaries of property right. And in the face of a politics that all too often adopts a posture of resignation in the face of a biospheric catastrophe, it is imperative that we do not give in to the sense of the inevitable. Neoliberalism has a vested interest in selective fatalism. Perhaps

then the task of a counterpolitics is two-fold: wherever possible, all efforts should be made to undermine the foregone conclusion, and when all else fails, the aim should be to reroute the catastrophe toward more interesting ends (catastrophes often become the occasion for renewing and creating countercommunities). (p. 99)

Cooper's call is to rewire the future materially, affectively and symbolically, to imbue it with a frame and atmosphere of living with difference and uncertainty that strives for non-calamitous and solidaristic ends. She does not spell out the detail of such a politics of rerouting, but the options are not hard to imagine, and certainly need to spread as new public desires, if the visceral grip of the apocalyptic imaginary is to be loosened, and if a new vitalism with its own material culture is to become a form of second nature (Coole and Frost, 2010). Some counter-arrangements are already in place, though struggling for voice and expansion (cf. Amin and Thrift, 2012). For example, experiments in techno-democracy, from open-source code and anti-profiling software, to attempts to ensure genetic justice and monitor nature's laments, provide ways of imagining and facilitating new futures, modelling probabilities in alternative ways, and pushing against the technologies of calamity and calamitous organization (Pickering, 2010). Similarly, in the interstices of the corporate or cut-throat economy, experiments persist in social enterprise, ethical trade, alternative finance, non-monetary exchange, public ownership, profit-sharing, corporate social responsibility, social accounting, quality branding, ethical investment, responsible banking and minimum-risk securitization. This persistence signals the possibility of the plural, carefully audited and non-profligate economy, and also the follies of tackling risk by taking risk. Then, too, a raft of practices for the shared global commons exist, opposed to selective and divisive fatalism. They range from experiments of empowerment, redistribution and protection to enhance global social justice and solidarity, to interventions such as sustainable farming, energy conservation and aggressive legislative monitoring to conserve the ecological commons.

This mere hint of possibility endorses another politics of life, one far from assured in the struggle against the might of the security-entertainment complex and other weapons of catastrophism. But the very evidence of counter-organization is proof of the possibility of another way of working in the future, of reappraising the nostra of risk management that have come to the fore. They provide reason to push back at the belief that the only path that can arise out of the ashes of the post-war model of knowing and underwriting the future is that of the vigilant, resilient and combative subject, and show that the discourse of Apocalypse also rests on fragile foundations (Hardt and Negri, 2009). They prepare the ground for a politics of the midfield, one that drops the pretence of mastering the future by jumping on the back of one of the four horses to sweep aside anything that gets in the way, and instead doing everything humanly possible to minimize disturbances that generate violent breaches and disastrous tipping points. Advancing such cause will require the automation of many safeguards: a culture of caution and precaution, an extensive infrastructure of checks and balances, courage to act on probabilistic calculations well before the tipping point, diplomatic negotiation of the strange and unknown and not its aggressive denial, and extensive expertise in areas that may lead to injurious fracture.

Above all, it will mean rethinking the meaning of preparedness for a turbulent future. Today, it has come to signify – at least in the neoliberal world – preparing for the worst and aggressively pushing back at identifiable sources of harm, while accepting that some sacrifices are inevitable (usually the vulnerable and undefended). This thinking needs to be reversed, by adding more anticipatory and protective measures to the available arsenal, by minimizing the potential of damage and maximizing the capacity to resist and recover. If such thinking takes us back to arguments for central planning and state responsibility, extensive expertise, comprehensive insurance and protection, precautionary and peaceful action, automated maintenance and repair, and protecting the interests of the vulnerable, let it do so, without temptation to be apologetic, ashamed about some putative return to an age of centrism. Without these kinds of progress, the society of strangers will implode, or, more accurately, eliminate everything that smells of difference.

Proposals for democratization, such as those in science and technology studies recommending technologies of humility, publicly debated controversies and pluralist decision-making, make sense if the central authorities can be held to keep their side of the bargain in a new precautionary and provisioning culture of risk management. Only then will new ways of mapping and addressing hazard and risk reference each other (Whatmore, 2009) in the spirit of 'creative sabotage of the future' (Cooper, 2008), resisting the easy response to threat by those in power to crush the stranger, the weak and vulnerable, or democracy itself. The political uses of doom to reimpose centred power will not fritter away, for a lot is being achieved in its name. They will continue to silence any appeal for reasonableness in the scramble for survival, which is why the automation of democracy, including keeping the authorities in check and demanding that they play their part in a non-inflammatory politics of civil protection, remains so important.

If Peter Sloterdijk (2010) is right to describe ours as a time of rage and hysterical suspicion between peoples, following the release of innate human furies by the collapse of societal disciplines such as communism and Catholicism, new means of moderation must arise if the enmity between strangers is to be kept in check. Perhaps this will come, as Sloterdijk suggests (p. 229), from building skills of diplomacy based on 'learning to see oneself always through the eyes of others' and developing an 'anti-authoritarian morality' of intercultural engagement. But it will also come from building diplomacy into the machinery of risk management itself, so that catastrophism and its damaging selections is dismantled by the machinery of risk mitigation, by the rules of permissible action and collective organization.

Epilogue

Today's geopolitical and biopolitical circumstances, enveloped by calamitous imaginaries and sentiments, do not make for a fair politics of the stranger. Yet they do not fully colonize the settlements of situated practice. There continue to persist the bridges of collaborative work, the reconciliations of urban co-presence, the ties born in friendship and through material intimacies, as does the quest in many parts of the world for security, peace and well-being. These remainders speak to a politics of the provisioning commons, crafts of diplomacy and democratic deliberation, sentiments of fairness, care and responsibility, and interest in the open and plural society. The land of strangers may have become a rough place, but not without unease, without desire for another way of living with difference and turbulence.

The remarkable chain of calamities that framed the first half of 2011, under the shadow of which this epilogue was drafted, are testament to these ambiguities. In Egypt, an urban populace inspired by change in Tunisia came out on the street and remained firm, bringing down an embedded dictatorship. Strangers became allies in the theatre of the square, supported by solidarities struck in the street and through digital technologies and the international media. The uprising forced a radical constitutional and political upheaval. It was a heady moment for revolutionaries and reformists alike; hymn to the power of mass rebuttal of poverty and injustice and to loyalties among strangers that can arise to demand a better world. But in the passing of the moment and the delegation of authority to an uncertain body of representative powers, the active public turned into a body of dependent citizens, unsure of the gains to come, reliant on the movements working in their name. The euphoria of revolutionary potentiality gave way to the nervous anxiety of expectant hope, the dread that much might not change as a people returned to being a populace struggling with the cares of daily survival, subject to the power play of elites new and old.

In Libya, the politics of the event turned out to be very different despite the similarity of grass-root conditions and feelings. The brutality of the Gaddafi regime and its ability to wield a politics of rout, fear and selective favours prevented the formation of a visible and united counter-public. A chain of solidarity could not form, certainly not one strong enough to instruct this travesty of a 'people's' government to pack its bags. It would take the theatre of war, and its balance of force between the regime, rebel militia, allied bombings and regional holdouts, to decide the outcome. The politics of civil war and international intervention, and not the politics of a united and vociferous public, would have the last word. Strangers who came together in diverse communities – territorial, political, ideological – were subjected to the calculations and strategies of deciding others. As the world at large blew hot and cold over the intentions and implications of the NATO-led incursion against Gaddafi, the formations of a mature politics of transition during the emergency could not go unnoticed. In regions beyond the control of the regime, publics, soldiers, city councils and civic leaders learned to work together to voice collective demands, defend their gains and cobble together the rules of democratic emergency management. Libya saw the stirrings of responsible government and non-vengeful politics, which has survived into the short period since the toppling of the Gaddafi regime (Stewart, 2011).

In Japan, the strain of two devastations flushed out a contradictory politics of care. On the one hand, the response to the tsunami/earthquake, though slow in delivering state and international aid to the most afflicted communities, told the tale of a country united in trying to pick up the pieces, dealing with the situation with dignity, and rebuilding as quickly as possible. The emergency services did what they could, though perhaps not quickly enough for the many who went for so long without relief. The tacit social contract between a providing state and a resilient public just about held together. There was no disintegration into feral warfare. But the handling of the Fukushima nuclear disaster revealed a very different politics of the moment. The combination of mawkish, hesitant and opaque response from the state and the owners of the nuclear plant strained Japan's social contract to the limit, leaving an angry and anxious public eager for reassurances. A once secure and trusting public lost its faith but still looked to the state to return Japan to normality, while the tainted authorities continued to behave as though the risky future could be secured. The two connected disasters simultaneously reinforced and shattered the politics of trust.

In the meantime, in the lands of vociferous publics and dissenting public cultures, the clamour of malcontent against government austerity measures in the wake of the global financial crisis was met with stony silence. The British government wrung its hands in sympathy with half a million people who protested in late March 2011 against its deep cuts in public expenditure, arguing that these were inevitable and necessary to restore growth. The protestors and the public were not reassured, but the government simply carried on, slashing here and slashing

there, distant from its own people and its material concerns, while embarking on a costly military intervention
in Libya in the name of protecting civilian freedom. Later
in the year, the government crushed the youth riots, refus-
ing to hear of any talk of the liberal way of life failing a
disenchanted urban population. In Portugal, and later
Greece, similar pleas against mass unemployment and
economic insecurity – short-term and long-term – fell on
deaf ears, as the European Union laid out its strict restrictions on state borrowing and expenditure to bail out the
economy. In all these countries, governments jittery in the
face of faltering markets and neoliberal orthodoxy found
themselves on the same side as the elites that caused or
prospered from the crisis, against the ordinary citizen.
They wittingly or otherwise broke the social contract,
turning swathes of their own citizens into the unwanted
or errant subject.

The extremes that announced 2011 exposed the limitations of authoritarian and unrepresentative government;
the fragilities of the revolutionary moment handed on,
the limits of the social contract between the trusted state
and the trusting public, the arrogances of centred power,
and the shortcomings of hollow democracy. Ironically,
in its brief march, the Libyan resistance, though clearly
without the means to secure livelihoods, drew strength
and legitimacy from casting the net of authority and
responsibility widely. The resistance movement became
the armed force, the governing body and the mobilized
people, expected to act decisively, draw on distributed
resilience and capability, maintain legitimacy, and deliver
a positive outcome.

In its own way, in articulating a pluralist politics of
difference mediated by a provisioning centre and an
amplified commons, this book has striven towards a
similar architecture of responsibility and care. Breaking
with the compulsions of community and interpersonal
recognition, and choosing instead the social state, distributed rights and obligations, the plural public sphere, and

collective labour, the book has invested in the principles of proliferation and overlap as the solution to frictions over difference and suspicions of insecurity and uncertainty. It has concluded that the interpersonal – and by extension care for each other and the community – play a small part in moderating the cohesiveness of the plural society. Instead, it has suggested that the balance between aversion and empathy, between inclusion and exclusion, is regulated by the many conditionings and contingencies of situated practice. Outcomes concerning the stranger have been explained in terms of the jostle between the provisions and projections of togetherness in the public sphere, the power of legacies of bodily judgement, the entanglements of care between humans and the object world, the habits of spatial dwelling, and the experiences of joint working. The frames of encounter, rather than the encounter itself, have been considered to be of central importance, as have been the terms of encounter. The argument has pushed in the direction of neutralizing inherited privileges of claim and status so that all are rendered strangers before the encounter, with a series of framing conditions that guide the event towards a progressive outcome (Humphrey, 2008).

Such a politics of the encounter alone will not deliver the society that values the stranger. But it will help to close in on narrow ends, defensive postures and exclusionary reflexes, not because the right and the just will suddenly jump into view, but because multiplicity and common endeavour will have been put in place as political conducts fit for both fair and turbulent times. There will be no waiting for love between strangers, the clearances of symbolic divestiture or revolution, or the Truth Event, before moving towards such a polity (Rothenberg, 2010). There will be just the surety that the future cannot be approached in a heavy-handed way, that even the most urgent decision demands social legitimacy, and that negotiating an uncertain world requires all hands and capabilities. While this may not deliver the house on the hill, it may, as Boaventura

Santos (2009: 122) puts it, deliver a certain 'reasonableness in the will to fight for a better world and a more just
society, a set of ways of knowing and precarious calculations, animated by ethical exigencies and vital necessities'.
It is time to give a politics of reasonableness a chance, to
stop the politics of purge from ushering in the calamity it
purports to avoid.

Bibliography

Adenzato, M. and Garbarini, F. (2006) 'The *as if* in cognitive science, neuroscience and anthropology: a journey among robots, blacksmiths and neurons', *Theory and Psychology*, 16/6: 747–59.

Agamben, G. (2000) *Theory Out of Bounds*, Minneapolis, MN: University of Minnesota Press.

Agier, M. (2011) *Le couloir des exilés. Être étranger dans un monde commun*, Paris: Croquant Edition.

Ahluwalia, P. (2007) 'Afterlives of post-colonialism: reflections on theory post-9/11', *Postcolonial Studies*, 10/3: 257–70.

Ahmed, S. (2004) *The Cultural Politics of Emotion*, London: Routledge.

Ahmed, S. (2007) 'You end up doing the document rather than doing the doing: diversity, race equality and the politics of documentation', *Ethnic and Racial Studies*, 30/4: 390–609.

Alcoff, L. (2006) *Invisible Identities*, New York: Oxford University Press.

Alexander, C. (2004) 'Imagining the Asian gang: ethnicity, masculinity and youth after "the riots"', *Critical Social Policy*, 24/4: 526–49.

Amin, A. (2002) 'Ethnicity and the multicultural city', *Environment and Planning A*, 34/6: 959–80.

Amin, A. (2004) 'Multiethnicity and the idea of Europe', *Theory Culture and Society*, 21/2: 1–24.

Amin, A. (2007) 'Rethinking the urban social', *City*, 11/1: 100–14.

Amin, A. (2008) 'Collective culture and urban public space', *City*, 12/1: 5–24.

Amin, A. (2010) 'The remainders of race', *Theory, Culture and Society*, 27/1: 1–23.

Amin, A. (2011) 'Urban planning in an uncertain world'. In G. Bridge and S. Watson (eds), *The New Blackwell Companion to the City*, Oxford: Blackwell.

Amin, A. and P. Cohendet (2004). *Architectures of Knowledge: Firms, Capabilities, and Communities*, Oxford: Oxford University Press.

Amin, A. and J. Roberts (2008a) 'Knowing in action: beyond communities of Practice', *Research Policy*, 37/2: 353–69.

Amin, A. and J. Roberts (eds) (2008b) *Community, Economic Creativity and Organisation*, Oxford: Oxford University Press.

Amin, A. and N. Thrift (2002) *Cities: Rethinking the Urban*, Cambridge: Polity.

Amin, A. with N. Thrift (2007) 'Cultural-economy and cities', *Progress in Human Geography*, 31: 143–61.

Amin, A. and N. Thrift (2012) *Political Openings: Recovering Left Political Will*, Durham, NC: Duke University Press, in press.

Amoore, L. and A. Hall (2009) 'Taking people apart: digitised dissection and the body at the border', *Environment and Planning D: Society and Space*, 27: 444–64.

Anderson, B. (2010) 'Preemption, precaution, preparedness: anticipatory action and future geographies', *Progress in Human Geography*, 34: 777–98.

Anderson, B. (2012) 'Affect and biopower: towards a politics of life', *Transactions of the Institute of British Geographers*, 37/1: 28–43.

Anderson, P. (2007) 'Depicting Europe', *London Review of Books*, 29/18: 13–21.

Antonsich, M. (2008) 'European attachment and meanings of Europe. A qualitative study in the EU-15', *Political Geography*, 27: 691–710.

Appadurai, A. (2006) *Fear of Small Numbers*, Durham, NC: Duke University Press.

Appiah, A. (2006) *Cosmopolitanism*, London: Penguin.

Asad, T. (2003) *Formations of the Secular*, Stanford, CA: Stanford University Press.

Azmanova, A. (2012) *The Scandal of Reason*, New York: Columbia.

Bailey, F. G. (1996) *The Civility of Indifference*, Ithaca, NY: Cornell University Press.

Balibar, E. (2004) *We, the People of Europe?* Princeton, NJ: Princeton University Press.

Balibar, E. (2011) 'Our European incapacity', *OpenDemocracy*, 16 May, at: ⟨http://www.opendemocracy.net/etienne-balibar/our-european-incapacity⟩.

Barry, A. and N. Thrift (2007) 'Gabriel Tarde: imitation, invention and economy', *Economy and Society*, 36/4: 509–25.

Bartkowski, F. (2008) *Kissing Cousins: A New Kinship Bestiary*, New York: Columbia University Press.

Bathelt, H., A. Malmberg and P. Maskell (2004) 'Clusters and knowledge: local buzz, global pipelines and the process of knowledge creation', *Progress in Human Geography*, 28/1: 54–79.

Bauman, Z. (2000) *Liquid Modernity*, Cambridge: Polity.

Bauman, Z. (2004) *Europe: An Unfinished Adventure*. Cambridge: Polity.

Bauman, Z. (2007) *Liquid Times: Living in an Age of Uncertainty*, Cambridge: Polity.

Baumeister, A. (2007) 'Diversity and unity: the problem with "Constitutional Patriotism"', *European Journal of Political Theory*, 6: 483–503.

Bayart, J-F. (2005) *The Illusion of Identity*, Chicago, IL: University of Chicago Press.

Beck, U. (2002) 'The cosmopolitan society and its enemies', *Theory, Culture and Society*, 19/1–2: 17–44.

Beck, U. and E. Grande (2007) 'Cosmopolitanism: Europe's way out of crisis', *European Journal of Social Theory*, 10: 67–85.

Benkler, Y. (2006) *The Wealth of Networks*, New Haven, CT: Yale University Press.

Bennett, J. (2001) *The Enchantment of Modern Life*, Princeton, NJ: Princeton University Press.

Bennett, J. (2010) *Vibrant Matter: A Political Economy of Things*, Durham, NC: Duke University Press.

Berlant, L. (2008) *The Female Complaint*, Durham, NC: Duke University Press.

Bernasconi, R. and T. Lott (2000) *The Idea of Race*, Indianapolis, IN: Hackett.

Beunza, D. and D. Stark, (2004) 'Tools of the trade: the sociotechnology of arbitrage in a Wall Street trading room', *Industrial and Corporate Change*, 13/2: 369–400.

Boase, J., J. Horrigan, B. Wellman and L. Raine (2006) *The Strength of Internet Ties*, Washington, DC: Pew Internet and American Life Project.

Bollens, S. A. (2007) *Cities, Nationalism and Democratization*, London: Routledge.

Boltanski, L. and L. Thévenot (2006) *On Justification: The Economies of Worth*, Princeton, NJ: Princeton University Press.

Borch, C. (2005) 'Urban imitations: Tarde's sociology revisited', *Theory, Culture and Society*, 22/3: 81–100.

Bowker, G. and S. Leigh Star (1999) *Sorting Things Out*, Cambridge, MA: MIT Press.

Brand, R. (2009) 'Urban artefacts and social practices in a contested city', *Journal of Urban Technology*, 16/2: 35–60.

Brown, W. (2006) *Regulating Aversion*, Princeton, NJ: Princeton University Press.

Brubaker, R., M. Loveman and P. Stamatov (2004) 'Ethnicity as cognition', *Theory and Society*, 33: 31–64.

Çalişcan, K. and M. Callon (2009) 'Economization, part 1: shifting attention from the economy towards processes of economization', *Economy and Society*, 38/3: 369–98.

Çalişcan, K. and M. Callon (2010) 'Economization, part 2: a research programme for the study of markets', *Economy and Society*, 39/1: 1–32.

Callon, M., P. Lascoumes and Y. Barthe (2009) *Acting in an Uncertain World*, Cambridge, MA: MIT Press.

Callon, M., C. Mèadel and A. Rabeharisoa (2002) 'The economy of qualities', *Economy and Society*, 31/2: 194–217.

Camilleri, J. A. (2008) 'Europe between Islam and the United States: interests, identity and geopolitics', *Global Change, Peace and Security*, 20/1: 9–24.

Carlile, P. R. (2002) 'A pragmatic view of knowledge and boundaries: boundary objects in new product development', *Organization Science*, 13/4: 442–55.

Carter, R. (2007) 'Genes, genomes and genealogies: the return of scientific racism?', *Ethnic and Racial Studies*, 30/4: 546–56.

Castells, M (2009) *Communication Power*, Oxford: Oxford University Press

Castree, N. (2005) *Nature*, London: Routledge.

CCCB (2007) *Apartheid*, Barcelona: Centre for Contemporary Culture Barcelona.

Cesarino, C. (2008) 'Surplus common: a preface'. In C. Cesarino and A. Negri (2008), *In Praise of the Common: A Conversation on Philosophy and Politics*, Minneapolis, MN: Minnesota University Press.

Chambers, D. (2006) *New Social Ties*, Basingstoke: Palgrave Macmillan.

Chambers, I. (2001) *Culture After Humanism*, London: Routledge.

Chambers, I. (2010) 'Maritime criticisms and lessons from the seas', *Insights*, 3/9: ⟨http://www.dur.ac.uk/ias/insights/volume3/article9/⟩.

Clark, A. (2007) 'Understanding community: a review of networks, ties and contacts', Leeds: ESRC National Centre for Research Methods, University of Leeds, NCRM Working Paper Series, 9/07.

Collier, S. J. and A. Lakoff (2008) 'Distributed preparedness: the spatial logic of domestic security in the United States', *Environment and Planning D: Society and Space*, 26: 7–28.

Collins, H. (2001), 'Tacit knowledge, trust and the Q of sapphire', *Social Studies of Science*, 31/1: 71–85.

Connolly, W. (2005) *Pluralism*, Durham, NC: Duke University Press.

Connolly, W. (2008) *Capitalism and Christianity, American Style*, Durham, NC: Duke University Press.

Connolly, W. (2010) *A World of Becoming*, Durham, NC: Duke University Press.

Cook, S. and D. Yanow (1993) 'Culture and organizational learning', *Journal of Management Inquiry*, 2/4: 373–90.

Coole, D. and S. Frost (2010) 'Introducing the new materialisms'. In D. Coole and S. Frost (eds), *New Materialisms: Ontology, Agency and Politics*, Durham, NC: Duke University Press.

Cooper, M. (2008) *Life as Surplus: Biotechnology & Capitalism in the Neoliberal Era*, Seattle, Washington: University of Washington Press.

Creplet, F., O. Dupouet, F. Kern, B. Mehmanpazir and F. Munier (2001) 'Consultants and experts in management consulting firms', *Research Policy*, 30: 1517–35.

Cresswell, T. (2006) *On the Move*, London: Routledge.

Dalal, F. (2008) 'Institutions and racism: equality in the workplace. In S. Davison and J. Rutherford (eds), *Race, Identity and Belonging*, London: Lawrence and Wishart, pp. 123–40.

Dallmayr, F. (2010) 'Befriending the stranger: beyond the global politics of fear', mimeo, Notre Dame, IL: University of Notre Dame.

Damasio, A. (2003) *Looking for Spinoza*, New York: Harcourt.

Darling, J. (2009) Becoming bare life: asylum, hospitality and the politics of encampment, *Environment and Planning D: Society and Space*, 27: 649–65.

Degen, M., G. Rose and B. Basdas (2010) 'Bodies and everyday practices in designed urban environments', *Science Studies*, 23/2: 60–76.

de Goede, M. and S. Randalls (2009) 'Precaution, pre-emption: arts and technologies of the actionable future', *Environment and Planning D: Society and Space*, 27: 859–78.

DeLanda, M. (2006) *A New Philosophy of Society*, London: Continuum.

Delanty, G. (2003) *Community*, London: Routledge.

Delanty, G. and C. Rumford (2005) *Rethinking Europe*, London: Routledge.

Derrida, J. (1997) *The Politics of Friendship*, London: Verso.

Derrida, J. (2002) *On Cosmopolitanism and Forgiveness*, London: Routledge.

Dicken, P. (2003) *Global Shift*, London: Sage.

Dillon, M. (2008) 'Underwriting security', *Security Dialogue*, 39/2–3: 309–32.

Dillon, M. and J. Reid (2009) *The Liberal Way of War: Killing to Make Life Live*, London: Routledge.

Diprose, R., N. Stephenson, C. Mills, K. Race and G. Hawkins (2008) 'Governing the future: the paradigm of prudence in political technologies of risk management', *Security Dialogue*, 39: 267–88.

Dodge, M. and R. Kitchen (2004) 'Flying through code/space: the real virtuality of air travel', *Environment and Planning A*, 36: 195–211.

Duguid, P. (2005) ' "The art of knowing": social and tacit dimensions of knowledge and the limits of the community of practice', *Information Society*, 21/2: 109–18.

Duguid, P. (2008) 'Community of practice then and now'. In A. Amin and J. Roberts (eds), *Community, Economic Creativity and Organization*, Oxford: Oxford University Press, pp. 1–10.

Dunbar, R. (2004) *The Human Story*. London: Faber and Faber.

Duster, T. (2003) *Backdoor to Eugenics*, London: Routledge.

Edwards, K. (2001) 'Epistemic communities, situated learning and open source software development', *Working paper*, Denmark: Technical University of Denmark.

Ekström, A. (2011) 'Exhibiting disasters: mediation, historicity and spectatorship', mimeo, Stockholm: Department of History of Science and Technology, KTH Royal Institute of Technology.

Ellis, D., R. Oldridge and A. Vasconcelos (2004) 'Community and virtual community', *Annual Review of Information Sciences and Technology*, 38: 146–86.

European Commission (1997) *Racism and Xenophobia in Europe*, Eurobarometer Opinion Poll no 47.1, Luxembourg: European Commission.

European Commission (2007) *European Cultural Values*, Special Eurobarometer 278, Luxembourg: European Commission.

EUMC (2005) *Majorities' Attitudes Towards Minorities*, Vienna: European Monitoring Centre on Racism and Xenophobia.

European Union Agency for Fundamental Rights (2009) *European Union Minorities and Discrimination Survey*, Vienna: FRA.

Fanon, F. (1967) [1952] *Black Skin, White Masks*, New York: Grove.

Farías, I. and T. Bender (eds) (2010) *Urban Assemblages: How Actor-Network Theory Changes Urban Research*, New York: Routledge.

Fassin, D. and M. Pandolfi (eds) (2010) *Contemporary States of Emergency: The Politics of Military and Humanitarian Interventions*, New York: Zone Books.

Fekete, L. (2004) Anti-Muslim racism and the European security state', *Race and Class*, 46/1: 3–29.

Fekete, L. (2009) *A Suitable Enemy: Racism, Migration and Islamophobia in Europe*, London: Pluto Press.

Fincher, R. and K. Iveson (2008) *Planning and Diversity in the City*, London: Palgrave Macmillan.

Fischer, G. (2001) 'Communities of interest: learning through the interaction of multiple knowledge systems', *Proceedings of the 24th IRIS Conference* (eds: S. Bjornestad, R. Moe, A. Morch, A. Opdahl), August 2001, Bergen, Norway: Ulvik, Department of Information Science, pp. 1–14.

Fortier, A-M. (2008) *Multicultural Horizons*, London: Routledge.

Foucault, M. (2003) *Society Must Be Defended*, London: Allen Lane.

Foucault, M. (2004) *Security, Territory, Population*, New York: Picador.

Frank, J. (2005) ' "Besides our selves": an essay on enthusiastic politics and civil subjectivity', *Public Culture*, 17/3: 371–92.

Franke, A. (ed.) (2005) *B-Zone: Becoming Europe and Beyond*, Berlin: Institute for Contemporary Art.

Fraser, N. (2005) 'Reframing global justice', *New Left Review*, NS, 36: 69–88.

Fullwiley, D. (2007) 'The molecularization of race: institutionalizing human difference in pharmacogenetics practice', *Science as Culture*, 16/1: 1–30.

Gandy, M. (2005) 'Cyborg urbanization: complexity and monstrosity in the contemporary city', *International Journal of Urban and Regional Research*, 29/1: 26–49.

Ghandi, L. (2006) *Affective Communities*, Durham, NC: Duke University Press.

Gherardi, S. (2009) 'Practice? It's a matter of taste!', *Management Learning*, 40/5: 535–50.

Gilroy, P. (2001) *Against Race*, Cambridge, MA: Belknap.

Gilroy, P. (2004) *After Empire: Melancholia or Convivial Culture?* London: Routledge.

Grabher, G. (2004) 'Temporary architectures of learning: knowledge governance in project ecologies', *Organization Studies*, 25/9: 1491–1514.

Grabher, G. and O. Ibert (2006) 'Bad company? The ambiguity of personal knowledge networks'. *Journal of Economic Geography*, 6: 251–71.

Graham, S. (2002) 'FlowCity: networked mobilities and the contemporary metropolis', *Journal of Urban Technology*, 9/1: 1–20.

Graham, S. (2010) *Cities Under Siege: The New Military Urbanism*, London: Verso.

Graham, S. and S. Marvin (2001) *Splintering Urbanism: Networked Infrastructures, Technological Mobilities and the Urban Condition*, London: Routledge.

Graham, S. and N. Thrift (2007) 'Out of order: understanding repair and maintenance, *Theory, Culture and Society*, 24: 1–25.

Grandadam, D., P. Cohendet and L. Simon (2009) 'Places, spaces and the dynamics of creativity: the video game industry in Montreal', *Regional Studies*, forthcoming.

Gregory, D. (2004) *The Colonial Present*, Oxford: Blackwell.

Gregson, N. (2009) 'Material, literary narrative and cultural economy', *Journal of Cultural Economy* 2/3: 285–300.

Grosz, E. (2004) *The Nick of Time*, Durham, NC: Duke University Press.

Habermas, J. (1996) *Between Facts and Norms: Contribution to a Theory of Law and Democracy*, Cambridge MA: MIT Press.

Habermas, J. (2009) *Europe: The Faltering Project*, Cambridge: Polity.

Hacking, I. (2005) 'Why race still matters', *Daedalus*, 134/1: 102–16.

Hacking, I. (2007) 'Our neo-Cartesian bodies in parts', *Critical Inquiry*, 34 (autumn): 78–105.

Hage, G. (1998) *White Nation*, Annandale, NSW: Pluto Press.

Hall, H. and D. Graham (2004) 'Creation and recreation: motivating collaboration to generate knowledge capital in online communities', *International Journal of Information Management*, 24: 235–46.

Hansen, P. (2009) 'Post-national Europe – without cosmopolitan guarantees', *Race & Class*, 50/4: 20–37.

Haraway, D. (1991) *Simians, Cyborgs and Women: The Reinvention of Nature*, New York: Routledge.

Hardt, M. and A. Negri (2009) *Commonwealth*, Cambridge, MA: Belknap.

Hariman, R. (1995) *Political Style*, Chicago, IL: Chicago University Press.

Hariman, R. (2009a) 'Cultivating compassion as a way of seeing', *Communication and Critical/Cultural Studies*, 6/2: 199–203.

Hariman, R. (2009b) 'Democratic stupidity', *Insights*, 2/14; available at: ⟨http://www.dur.ac.uk/ias/insights/volume2/article14/⟩.

Harris, N. (2002) *Thinking the Unthinkable*, London: Tauris and Co.

Hart, K., J-L. Laville and D. Cattani (eds) (2010) *The Human Economy*, Cambridge: Polity.

Herzog, D. (2006) *Cunning*, Princeton, NJ: Princeton University Press.

Heynen, N., M. Kaïka and E. Swyngedouw (eds) (2006) *The Nature of Cities: Urban Political Ecology and the Politics of Urban Metabolism*, London: Routledge.

Hinchliffe, S. and S. Whatmore (2006), 'Living cities: towards a politics of conviviality', *Science as Culture*, 15/2: 123–38.

Hirschfeld, L. (1996) *Race in the Making: Cognition, Culture and the Child's Conception of Human Kinds*, Cambridge, MA: MIT Press.

Honig, B. (2009) *Emergency Politics: Paradox, Law, Democracy*, Princeton, NJ: Princeton University Press.

Hughes, G. (2007) 'Community cohesion, asylum seeking and the question of the 'stranger'', *Cultural Studies*, 21/6: 931–51.

Humphrey, C. (2008) 'Reassembling individual subjects: events and decisions in troubled times', *Anthropolical Theory*, 8: 357–80.

Ingold, T. (2006) 'Rethinking the animate, re-animating thought', *Ethnos*, 71/1: 9–20.

Jacobs, J. (1961) *The Death and Life of Great American Cities*, New York: Random House.

James, W. (2003) *A Pluralistic Universe*, Nebraska: University of Nebraska Press.

Jasanoff, S. (2010) 'Beyond calculation: a democratic response to risk'. In A. Lakoff (ed.), *Disaster and the Politics of Intervention*, New York: Columbia University Press.

Johnson, C. M. (2001) 'A survey of current research on online communities of practice', *Internet and Higher Education*, 4: 45–60.

Johnson, M. (2006) 'Mind incarnate: from Dewey to Damasio', *Daedalus*, 135/ 3: 46–64.

Josefsson, U. (2005) 'Coping with illness online: the case of patients' online communities', *Information Society*, 21: 143–53.

Keith, M. (2005) *After the Cosmopolitan*, London: Routledge.

Klein, N. (2008) *The Shock Doctrine*, London: Penguin.

Kling, R. and C. Courtright (2003) 'Group behavior and learning in electronic forums: a sociotechnical approach', *Information Society*, 19: 221–35.

Knorr Cetina, K. (1999) *Epistemic Cultures: How the Sciences Make Sense*. Chicago, IL: Chicago University Press.

Knorr Cetina, K. (2005) 'Complex global microstructures: the new terrorist societies', *Theory, Culture and Society*, 22/5: 213–34.

Knorr Cetina, K. and U. Bruegger (2002a) 'Global microstructures: the virtual societies of financial markets', *American Journal of Sociology*, 107/4: 905–95.

Knorr Cetina, K. and U. Bruegger (2002b) 'Inhabiting technology: the global lifeform of financial markets', *Current Sociology*, 50: 389–405.

Kogut, B. and J. M. Macpherson (2004) 'The decision to privatize as an economic policy idea: epistemic communities, palace wars, and diffusion', mimeo, Paris: ISEAD.

Kohler-Koch, B. (2009) 'The three worlds of European civil society – what role for civil society for what kind of Europe?', *Policy & Society*, 28: 47–57.

Kristeva, J. (1993) *Nations without Nationalism*, New York: Columbia University Press.

Kumar, K. (2008) 'The question of European identity: Europe in the American mirror', *European Journal of Social Theory*, 11: 87–105.

Kundnani, A. (2007) *The End of Tolerance*, London: Pluto Press.

Kurth, J. (2006) 'Europe's identity problem and the new Islamist war', *Orbis* (summer): 541–57.

Laclau, E. (2005) *On Populist Reason*, London: Verso.

Lacroix, J. (2009) 'Does Europe need common values? Habermas vs Habermas', *European Journal of Political Theory*, 8/2: 141–56.

Lakoff, A. (2007) 'Preparing for the next emergency', *Public Culture*, 12/2: 247–71.

Lancione, M. (2011) 'Homeless subjects and the chance of space', unpublished PhD dissertation, Durham: Department of Geography, Durham University.

Landau, L. B. (2010) 'Inclusion in shifting sands: rethinking mobility and belonging in African cities'. In C. Kihato, M.

Massoumi, B. Ruble, P. Subirós and P. A. Garland (eds), *Inclusive Cities: The Challenge of Diversity*, Washington, DC: Woodrow Wilson Center Press.

Latham, A. and D. McCormack (2004) 'Moving cities: rethinking the materialities of urban geographies', *Progress in Human Geography*, 26/6: 701–24.

Latour, B. (2004a) 'Whose cosmos, which cosmopolitics? Comments on the peace terms of Ulrich Beck', *Common Knowledge*, 10/3: 450–62.

Latour, B. (2004b) *Politics of Nature: How to Bring the Sciences into Democracy*, Cambridge, MA: Harvard University Press.

Latour, B. (2005) *Reassembling the Social: An Introduction to Actor-Network Theory*, Oxford: Oxford University Press.

Latour, B. and P. Weibel (eds) (2005) *Making Things Public: Atmospheres of Democracy*, Cambridge, MA: MIT Press.

Lave, J. (2008) '*Situated Learning* and changing practice'. In A. Amin and J. Roberts (eds), *Community, Economic Creativity and Organization*, Oxford: Oxford University Press, pp. 283–96.

Lave, J. and E. Wenger (1991) *Situated Learning: Legitimate Peripheral Participation*. Cambridge: Cambridge University Press.

Lazzarato, M. (2004) *Les Révolutions de capitalisme*, Paris: Les Empêcheurs de Penser en Rond.

Lefebvre, H. (1996) *Writings on Cities*, trans. and ed. E. Kofman and E. Lebas, Oxford: Blackwell.

Lentin, A. (2008) 'Europe and the silence about race', *European Journal of Social Theory*, 11/4: 487–503.

Lentzos, F. and N. Rose (2009) 'Governing insecurity: contingency planning, protection, resilience', *Economy and Society*, 38/2: 230–54.

Levinas, E. (1998) *Entre Nous: On Thinking of the Other*, New York: Columbia University Press.

Lim, J. (2010) 'Queer politics and the politics of affect'. In B. Anderson and P. Harrison (eds), *Taking-Place: Non-Representational Theories and Geography*, London: Ashgate.

Lindkvist, L. (2005) 'Knowledge communities and knowledge collectivities: a typology of knowledge work in groups', *Journal of Management Studies*, 42/6: 1189–210.

McFarlane, C. (2010) 'Governing the contaminated city: infrastructure and sanitation in colonial and postcolonial Bombay',

International Journal of Urban and Regional Research, 32: 415–35.

McFarlane, C. (2011) *Learning the City: Translocal Assemblage and Urban Politics*, Oxford: Blackwell.

McLure-Wasko, M. and S. Faraj (2000) ' "It is what one does": why people participate and help others in electronic communities of practice', *Journal of Strategic Information Systems*, 9: 155–73.

Mamdani, M. (2004) *Good Muslim, Bad Muslim*, New York: Pantheon Books.

Marshall, C. C., F. M. Shipman III and R. J. McCall (1995) 'Making large-scale information resources serve communities of practice', *Journal of Management Information Systems*, 11/4: 65–86.

Martino, S. (2002) *The Rule of Racialization*, Philadelphia, PA: Temple University Press.

Marvin, S., and W. Medd (2006), 'Metabolisms of obesity: flows of fat through bodies, cities, and sewers', *Environment and Planning* A 38/2: 313–24.

Massey, D. (2005) *For Space*, London: Sage.

Massumi, B. (2009) 'National enterprise emergency: steps towards an ecology of powers', *Theory, Culture and Society*, 26: 153–85.

Mateos-Garcia, J. and W. E. Steinmueller (2008) 'Open but how much? Growth, conflict and institutional evolution in open-source communities'. In A. Amin and J. Roberts (eds), *Community, Economic Creativity and Organization*, Oxford: Oxford University Press, pp. 254–82.

Mbembe, A. (2008) 'Aesthetics of superfluity'. In S. Nuttall and A. Mbembe (eds), *Johannesburg: The Elusive Metropolis*, Durham, NC: Duke University Press.

Mendieta, E. (2011) 'Interspecies cosmopolitanism', *Logos*, 10/1; available at: ⟨http://www.logosjournal.com/interspecies-cosmopolitanism.php⟩.

Mendieta, E. (ed.) (forthcoming) *Biopolitics and Racism: Foucauldian Genealogies*, New York: SUNY Press.

Mignolo, W. D. (2009) 'Epistemic disobedience, independent thought and decolonial freedom', *Theory, Culture & Society*, 26: 159–81.

Miller, D. (2008) *The Comfort of Things*, Cambridge: Polity.

Miller, D. (2010) *Stuff*, Cambridge: Polity.

Mitchell, T. (2008) 'Rethinking economy', *Geoforum*, 39: 1116–21.

Modood, T. (2005) *Multicultural Politics: Racism, Ethnicity and Muslims in Britain*, Minneapolis, MN: University of Minnesota Press.

Morley, D. (2006) *Media, Modernity and Technology: The Geography of the New*, London: Routledge.

Naidoo, R. (2008) 'Fear of difference/fear of sameness: the road to conviviality'. In S. Davison and J. Rutherford (eds), *Race, Identity and Belonging*, London: Lawrence and Wishart, pp. 72–81.

Nally, D. (2011) *Human Encumbrances*, Notre Dame, IL: University of Notre Dame Press.

Nancy, J-L. (1993) *The Experience of Freedom,* Stanford, CA: Stanford University Press.

Nancy, J-L. (2000), *Being Singular Plural*, Stanford, CA: Stanford University Press.

Nederveen Pieterse, J. (2007) *Ethnicities and Global Multiculture*, Plymouth: Rowman and Littlefield.

Ngai, S. (2005) *Ugly Feelings*, Cambridge, MA: Harvard University Press.

Noble, G. (2009a) 'Where the bloody hell are we? Multicultural manners in a world of hyperdiversity'. In G. Noble (ed.), *Lines in the Sand: The Cronulla Riots and the Limits of Australian Multiculturalism*, Sydney: Institute of Criminology Press.

Noble, G. (2009b) 'Everyday cosmopolitanism and the labour of intercultural community'. In A. Wise and S. Velayutham (eds), *Everyday Multiculturalism*, Basingstoke: Palgrave Macmillan, pp. 46–65.

Olsson, G. (2007) *Abysmal*, Chicago, IL: Chicago University Press.

O'Malley, P. (2010) 'Resilient subjects: uncertainty, warfare and liberalism', *Economy and Society*, 39/4: 488–509.

Ophir, A. (2007) 'The two-state solution: providence and catastrophe', *Journal of Homeland Security and Emergency Management*, 4/1: 1–44.

Ophir, A. (2010) 'The politics of catastrophization: emergency and exception'. In D. Fassin and M. Pandolfi (eds), *Contemporary States of Emergency: The Politics of Military and Humanitarian Interventions*, New York: Zone Books, pp. 59–88.

Ophir, A. (2011) 'Power and catastrophes: reflections on immanence and exteriority', mimeo, Tel Aviv: Cohn Institute for
the History and Philosophy of Science and Ideas, Tel Aviv
University.

O'Riordan, T. and T. Lenton (2011) 'Tackling tipping points',
British Academy Review, 18 (summer): 21–7.

Orr, J. E. (1996). *Talking about Machines: An Ethnography of
a Modern Job*. Ithaca, NY, and London: IRL Press.

Outhwaite, W. (2008) *European Society*, Cambridge: Polity.

Pahl, R. (2000) *On Friendship*, Cambridge: Polity.

Parekh, B. (2000) *Rethinking Multiculturalism*, Basingstoke:
Palgrave.

Parekh, B. (2008) *A New Politics of Identity*, Basingstoke:
Palgrave.

Pearce, F. (2010) *The Climate Files*, London: Guardian Books.

Peck, J. (2010) *Constructions of Neoliberal Reason*, Oxford:
Oxford University Press.

Pescosolido, B. and B. Rubin (2000) 'The web of group affiliations revisited: postmodernism and sociology', *American
Sociological Review*, 65/1: 52–76.

Pichler, F. (2008) 'How real is cosmopolitanism in Europe?',
Sociology, 42/6: 1107–26.

Pickering, A. (1995) *The Mangle of Practice*, Chicago, IL: University of Chicago Press.

Pickering, A. (2010) *The Cybernetic Brain: Sketches of Another
Future*, Chicago, IL: Chicago University Press.

Pieterse, J. N. (2003) *Globalization and Culture*, New York:
Rowman and Littlefield.

Pile, S. (2005) *Real Cities*, London: Sage.

Povinelli, E. (2006) *The Empire of Love*, Durham, NC: Duke
University Press.

Power, D. (2010) 'The difference principle? Shaping competitive
advantage in the cultural product industries', *Geografiska
Annaler B*, 92/2: 1–14.

Pred, A. (2004) *The Past is not Dead*, Minneapolis, MN: University of Minnesota Press.

Pryke, M. (2010) 'Money's eyes: the visual preparation of financial markets', *Economy and Society*, 39/4: 427–59.

Rai, A. (2004) 'Of monsters: biopower, terrorism and excess in
genealogies of monstrosity', *Cultural Studies*, 18/4: 688–70.

Rankin, W. J. (2010) 'The epistemology of the suburbs: knowledge, production, and corporate laboratory design', *Critical Inquiry*, 36/4: 771–806.

Richardson, I., A. Third and I. MacColl (2007) 'Moblogging and belonging: new mobile phone practices and young people's sense of social interaction', *ACM International Conference Proceedings Series*, 274: 73–8.

Ricoeur, P. (1994) *Oneself as Another*, Chicago, IL: University of Chicago Press.

Rose, N. (1999) *Powers of Freedom*, Cambridge: Cambridge University Press.

Rose, N. (2007) *The Politics of Life Itself*, Princeton, NJ: Princeton University Press.

Rothenberg, M. A. (2010) *The Excessive Subject*, Cambridge: Polity.

Roy, A. (2009) 'Civic governmentality: the politics of inclusion in Beirut and Mumbai, *Antipode*, 41/1: 159–79.

Rozario, K. (2007) *Culture of Calamity*, Chicago, IL: University of Chicago Press.

Runciman, D. (2008) *Political Hypocrisy*, Princeton, NJ: Princeton University Press.

Rutherford, J. (2007) *After Identity*, London: Lawrence and Wishart.

Saldanha, A. (2006) 'Re-ontologizing race: the machinic geography of phenotype', *Environment and Planning D: Society and Space*, 24: 9–24.

Saldanha, A. (2007) *Psychedelic Whiteness: Rave Tourism and the Viscosity of Race in Goa*, Minneapolis, MN: University of Minnesota Press.

Sandercock, L. (2003) *Cosmopolis II*, London: Continuum.

Santos, B. S. (2009) 'A non-occidentalist West? Learned ignorance and ecology of knowledge', *Theory, Culture and Society*, 26: 103–25.

Sardar, Z. (2009) *Balti Britain: A Journey through the British Asian Experience*, London: Granta.

Sardar, Z. (2010) 'Welcome to postnormal times', *Futures*, 42/5: 435–44.

Sassen, S. (ed.) (2002) *Global Networks, Linked Cities*, London: Routledge.

Sassen, S. (2010) 'When the city itself becomes a technology of war', *Theory, Culture and Society*, 27: 33–50.

Seabright, P. (2005) *The Company of Strangers: The Natural History of Economic Life*, Princeton, NJ: Princeton University Press.

Sennett, R. (2008a) 'The public realm', paper presented at BMW Foundation Workshop on Changing Behaviour and Beliefs, BMW Foundation, Lake Tegernsee, 17–21 July 2008.

Sennett, R. (2008b) *The Craftsman*, London: Allen Lane.

Shapiro, M. (2010) *The Time of the City*, New York: Routledge.

Shehu, B. (2011) 'East European geographobia', *OpenDemocracy*, 11 May: ⟨http://www.opendemocracy.net/bashkim-shehu/east-european-geographobia⟩.

Simmel, G. (1964) *Conflict & The Web of Group-Affiliations*, New York: Free Press.

Simmel, G. (1970) 'The metropolis of modern life.' In D. Levine (ed.), *Simmel: On Individuality and Social Forms*, Chicago, IL: Chicago University Press.

Simone, A. (2008) 'People as infrastructure'. In S. Nuttall and A. Mbembe (eds), *Johannesburg: The Elusive Metropolis*, Durham, NC: Duke University Press.

Simone, A. (2010) *City Life from Jakarta to Dakar*, New York: Routledge.

Simone, A. (2011) 'The ambivalence of the arbitrary', *Theory, Culture and Society*, 28/1: 129–37.

Sloterdijk, P. (2005) *Esferas III, Espumas*, Barcelona: Editorial Siruela.

Sloterdijk, P. (2009) 'Airquakes', *Environment and Planning D: Society and Space*, 27: 41–57.

Sloterdijk, P. (2010) *Rage and Time*, New York: Columbia University Press.

Smith, A. (1759) *The Theory of Moral Sentiments*, London: Millar.

Solnit, R. (2009) *A Paradise Built in Hell*, New York: Viking.

Sparke, M. (2005) *In the Space of Theory*, Minnesota, MN: University of Minnesota Press.

Stark, D. (2009) *The Sense of Dissonance: Accounts of Worth in Economic Life*. Princeton, NJ: Princeton University Press.

Stark, D. (2010) 'What's valuable?', mimeo, New York: Department of Sociology, Columbia University.

Stewart, K. (2007) *Ordinary Affects*, Durham, NC: Duke University Press.

Stewart, R. (2011) 'Because we weren't there?', *London Review of Books*, 33/18, 22 (September): 11–12.

Stienen, A. (2009) 'Urban technology, conflict education and disputed space', *Journal of Urban Technology*, 16/2: 109–42.

Storper, M. (2008) 'Community and economics'. In A. Amin and J. Roberts (eds), *Community, Economic Creativity and Organization*, Oxford: Oxford University Press, pp. 37–68.

Strati, A. (1999) *Organization and Aesthetics*, London: Sage.

Subirós, P. (2011) 'Don't ask me where I'm from: thoughts of immigrants to Catalonia on social integration and cultural capital', *International Journal of Urban and Regional Research*, 35/2: 437–44.

Swan, J., H. Scarbrough and S. Newell (2010) 'Why don't (or do) organizations learn from projects?' *Management Learning*, 41: 325–44.

Swanton, D. (2007) 'Race and becoming: the Emergent Materialities of Race in Everyday Multiculture', unpublished PhD thesis, Durham: Department of Geography, University of Durham.

Swanton, D. (2010) 'Flesh, metal, road: tracing the machinic geographies of race', *Environment and Planning D: Society and Space*, 28/3: 447–66.

Swyngedouw, E. (2004) *Social Power and the Urbanization of Water: Flows of Power*, Oxford: Oxford University Press.

Szerszynski, B. and J. Urry (2010) 'Changing climates: Introduction', *Theory, Culture and Society*, 27/1: 1–8.

Tarde, G. (1989) [1890] *L'Opinion et la foule*, Paris: PUF.

Terranova, T. (2007) 'Futurepublic: on information warfare, bio-racism and hegemony as noopolitics', *Theory, Culture and Society*, 24/3: 125–45.

Thompson, E. P. (1980) 'Notes on exterminism, the last stage of civilization', *New Left Review*, 1/121: 3–31.

Thompson, M. (2005) 'Structural and epistemic parameters in communities of practice', *Organization Science*, 16/2: 151–64.

Thrift, N. (2005a) 'But malice aforethought: cities and the natural history of hatred', *Transactions of the Institute of British Geographers*, 30/2: 133–50.

Thrift, N. (2005b) *Knowing Capitalism*, London: Sage.

Thrift, N. (2008) 'Re-animating the place of thought: transformations of the spatial and temporal description of the twenty-first century', In A. Amin and J. Roberts (eds), *Community,*

Economic Creativity and Organization, Oxford: Oxford University Press, pp. 90–122.

Thrift, N. (2011) 'Lifeworld Inc – and what to do about it', *Environment and Planning D: Society and Space*, 29: 5–26.

Tilly, C. (2005) *Identities, Boundaries and Social Ties*, Boulder, CO: Paradigm.

Tobias, S. (2005) 'Foucault on freedom and capabilities', *Theory, Culture and Society*, 22/4: 65–85.

Todorov, T. (2010) *The Fear of Barbarians*, Cambridge: Polity.

Tolia-Kelly, D. (2010) *Landscape, Race and Memory: Material Ecologies of Home*, Farnham: Ashgate.

Toscano, A. (2007) 'Vital strategies: Maurizio Lazzarato and the metaphysics of contemporary capitalism', *Theory, Culture and Society*, 24/6: 71–91.

Tulchin, J. S. (2010) 'Crime and violence: the threat of division and exclusion in Latin American cities'. In C. Kihato, M. Massoumi, B. Ruble, P. Subirós and A. Garland (eds), *Inclusive Cities: The Challenge of Diversity*, Washington, DC: Woodrow Wilson Center Press.

Turnaturi, G. (2007) *Betrayals*, Chicago, IL: Chicago University Press.

Valentine, G. (2008) 'Living with difference: reflections on geographies of encounter', *Progress in Human Geography*, 32: 321–35.

Vergès, F. (2011) *L'Homme prédateur*, Paris: Albin Michel.

Vertovec, S. (2011) 'The cultural politics of nation and migration', *The Annual Review of Anthropology*, 40: 241–56.

Vertovec, S. and S. Wessendorf (eds) (2010) *The Multicultural Backlash*, London: Routledge.

Venn, C. (2010) 'Individuation, relationality, affect: rethinking the human in relation to the living', *Body & Society*, 16: 129–61.

Verstraete, G. (2010) *Tracking Europe: Mobility, Diaspora, and the Politics of Location*, Durham, NC: Duke University Press.

Wellman, B. (2001) 'Physical space and cyberspace: the rise of personalised networking', *International Journal of Urban and Regional Research*, 25: 227–52.

Wenger, E. (1998) *Communities of Practice: Learning, Meaning, and Identity*. Cambridge: Cambridge University Press.

Wenger, E. (2000) 'Communities of practice and social learning systems, *Organization*, 7/2: 225–46.

West, C. (2003) *Prophecy, Deliverance: An Afro-American Revolutionary Christianity*, Louisville, KY: Westminster/John Knox Press.

Whatmore, S. (2009) 'Mapping knowledge controversies: science, democracy and the redistribution of expertise', *Progress in Human Geography*, 33/5: 587–98.

Wilson, H. (2009) 'Encounter and the regulation of tolerance', mimeo, Durham: Department of Geography, Durham University.

Winant, H. (2006) 'Race and racism: towards a global future', *Ethnic and Racial Studies*, 29/5: 986–1003.

Wise, A. (2005) 'Hope and belonging in a multicultural suburb', *Journal of Intercultural Studies*, 26/1–2: 171–86.

Wise, A. (2009) 'Everyday multiculturalism: transversal crossings and working class cosmopolitans'. In A. Wise and S. Velayutham (eds), *Everyday Multiculturalism*, Basingstoke: Palgrave Macmillan, pp. 21–45.

Wise, A. (2010) 'Sensuous multiculturalism: emotional landscapes of inter-ethnic living in Australian suburbia', *Journal of Ethnic and Migration Studies*, 36/6: 917–37.

Wodak, R. (2011) *The Discourse of Politics in Action: Politics as Usual* (2nd revsd edn), Basingstoke: Palgrave.

Wood, P. and C. Landry (2007) *Intercultural City*, London: Earthscan.

Yanow, D. (2001) 'Learning in and from improvising: lessons from theater for organizational learning', *Reflections*, 2/4: 58–65.

Young, I. M. (2005) 'De-centering the project of global democracy'. In D. Lévy, M. Pensky and J. C. Torpey (eds), *Old Europe, New Europe, Core Europe*, London: Verso.

Žižek, S. (2008) *Violence*, London: Profile Books.

Žižek, S. (2010) *Living in the End Times,* London: Verso.

Index

Page numbers followed by 't' refer to a table, page numbers followed by 'n' refer to a note – e.g., 41t, 91n.